Idaho

MYTHS & LEGENDS

THE TRUE STORIES BEHIND HISTORY'S MYSTERIES

RANDY STAPILUS

Globe
Pequot

Guilford, Connecticut

Globe Pequot

An imprint of The Rowman & Littlefield Publishing Group, Inc.
4501 Forbes Blvd., Ste. 200
Lanham, MD 20706
www.rowman.com

Distributed by NATIONAL BOOK NETWORK

Map by Melissa Baker

British Library Cataloguing in Publication Information available

Library of Congress Cataloging-in-Publication Data available

ISBN 978-1-4930-4037-7 (paper : alk. paper)
ISBN 978-1-4930-4038-4 (electronic)

♾™ The paper used in this publication meets the minimum requirements of American National Standard for Information Sciences—Permanence of Paper for Printed Library Materials, ANSI/NISO Z39.48-1992.

CONTENTS

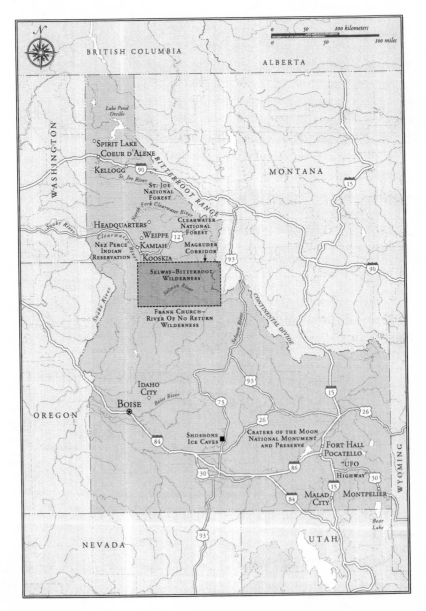

IDAHO

ACKNOWLEDGMENTS

A book may have one parent of record, but far more who stand in the background . . .

I received lots of help, as I have on other Idaho book projects, from a long list of Idahoans with deep background in the state. They include Judy Austin, Martin Peterson, Rick Just, Cort Conley, Steve Steubner, Ernest Hoidal, Jennifer Okerlund, Mark Mendiola, Tim Marsano, Sal Celeski, and Marty Trillhaase.

Many people helped with specific information in the various chapters. They include Dolli Massener, Dick Southern (thanks for help with both information and images), J. D. Williams (for sharing his personal story of Samaria Hills exploration) and the staff at the Shoshone Ice Caves (for their overall help and especially their tour of the place), the Boise City Department of Arts and History, and Radek Konarik at the Butch Cassidy Museum / the Bank of Montpelier.

David Bond, who's lived and reported in the Silver Valley so long he probably knows it better than it knows itself, helped greatly with the Noah Kellogg section (and thanks for his book loan). The report on "the Ridgerunner" would not have been practical, or at least comprehensible, without the groundwork done by my old newspaper colleague Rick Ripley, who wrote the book *The*

Ridgerunner. The good people at Big River Paranormal helped bring some perspective to the stories surrounding the old Idaho Penitentiary.

Thanks too to the fine editors at Globe Pequot Press.

And of course, my wife and chief proofreader, Linda Watkins.

INTRODUCTION

One of the oldest original Idaho documents in my collection is a little booklet, dating to somewhere around 1930, called "Copper Camp Mining Co., Inc.—A Prospectus." It was a call for investors, and so includes financial and technical information, but much of it reads like a short story from the dawn of the twentieth century—a short story without an ending.

It was written by William A. Edwards, a native of Georgia who became a lawyer for the General Land Office. He reported that "in 1901 my health broke down and I was compelled to resign and seek an outdoor life." The story generations later in Idaho was that the operative phrase there was "compelled to resign" and that his health actually was sound. He went on: "Because of my knowledge of mining law, I decided to go to some new mining camp in the Rocky Mountain States." In Spokane, he heard about fresh activity in the Thunder Mountain region in southwest Idaho—east of present-day McCall—and he ventured there to check for opportunities. He found none at first, but continued to prowl the nearby area, and soon came to Big Creek.

Big Creek is well known today by Idaho's backcountry enthusiasts as a spot an hour or so away from paved roads and telephone lines and on the very border of the Frank Church–

River of No Return Wilderness. Its human development includes a landing strip and a lodge and not much else. In 1904, Edwards saw not even any of these things, but he did perceive a massive mining opportunity, for gold, silver, and lead. That was the heart of his "prospectus."

There is today a tiny dot on some very fine-grained maps of Idaho marking a place called "Edwardsburg." It is located about a half mile from Big Creek; today, like Big Creek, it has a guest lodge and also several vacation homes, along with the ruins of the house Edwards built generations ago for his family. But although prospectors have occasionally wandered through and several small mines were developed in the surrounding hills, the Big Creek area never developed into a major mining center.

Locally, Edwards and his family became most identified with the old house, which returned to the ground after decades of abandonment. But for those who know the deep history of the place, Edwards became something of a legendary and even shadowy figure. He and his family were not quite hermits, but they rarely ventured into the outside world. Over the years, to raise money, Edwards would reach out to people trying to sell pieces of his property, but he became a figure of mystery. His reasons for leaving the General Land Office so long before are unclear; his protests of bad health didn't seem to converge with his ability to thrive—personally build a substantial house and seriously prospect for precious metals—in some of Idaho's most remote and tough backwoods country. What was he doing back there for so many years? What might he really have found?

He became a local legend, and is almost a figure of myth now. In another generation or two, his name will still be around . . . and who knows what may be said of him?

Idaho generates people like that.

As well it should. Idaho has a distant feel—"Silver and gold in the sunlight blaze, and romance lies in her name," runs the state song—a little elusive, always imperfectly understood, and in many ways anything but prosaic.

To the cartographer Karl Musser, Idaho is a myth and a legend. Or so he says. We will not be silenced, he writes on his website Fantasymaps.com: There's growing evidence that only forty-nine states are real, and "Idaho" is a fake.

Supposedly, he acknowledges, there are more than a million residents of Idaho. No matter, Musser wrote: "Some people have come forward and claimed that they were born and raised in 'Idaho.' But every single person who made this claim have been shown to be frauds and charlatans." The mapmakers who have drawn Idaho onto their national maps are biased, he said. And isn't it odd that so large a space has so few people—so many fewer than most other states?

Musser concluded: "We have much more material on this conspiracy, and we have yet to uncover one iota of evidence that Idaho has ever existed. All of the so-called 'evidence' is a mixture of falsifications, coercions, lies and exaggerations."

Karl Musser is not alone. Others around the Internet also proclaim the idea that Idaho is a mythical place, its unusual shape devised to separate actual states—such as Oregon and Wyoming— from each other. On a map.

Or—and this idea should be a favorite in a state where suspicion of government often reaches near-religious levels—there's also the theory that Idaho is a massive mind-control experiment: Cross the border into it, and your mind is taken over by nefarious forces. (The borders, presumably, are monitored by black helicopters.)

All of this, amusing as it might be, of course isn't accurate. I've lived in Idaho over a period of decades, and when not living there I've visited regularly, and I know a bunch of people who do live there today, and plenty of expatriates. The available evidence of Idaho's existence is respectably extensive. Congress considers it real enough to give its representatives two votes, and four in the Electoral College, which is not something it would do lightly.

However, there's no lack of argument within the state about things that are real or maybe are not. The line between fact and fiction in Idaho can blur at the edges; visit some of the people who have retreated to its backcountry, and you can get a serious education in that point.

Mind control actually is a subject that has been discussed with some regularity in the state. So has concern about the possibility of government-backed conspiracies. That earlier reference to black helicopters was not accidental; congressional candidates have spoken of them. There may be a reason so many episodes of the television series *The X-Files*, including the pilot, were set in the Pacific Northwest.

You can find these concerns too in newspaper headlines.

In 1947, the water supply in Lewiston, one of the state's oldest cities with some of its oldest and most worn infrastructure, was upgraded, and in the process fluoride was added to it. It was a relatively new technology, and no other city west of the Rocky Mountains had yet added it to the drinking water system (though some cities, like Nampa and St. Anthony, took advantage of natural fluoride in the system). Debates over fluoridation have persisted, and have appeared in various places around the country, but few people would argue now as they did then that the project was an effort to dull the residents' minds and surreptitiously mentally "medicate" them. (You might still get some takers on that in Idaho, though.)

Or consider the many reports in Idaho of mysterious objects falling from the sky.

In the 1990s, there were sightings of odd fibers, apparently nontoxic but nonetheless peculiar, dropped from the sky over a large area in southwest Idaho, not far from Boise. No one seemed able to figure out what the fibers were or where they came from.

Birds have fallen from the sky too. Not landed, in the usual avian manner, but dropped—en masse, like a flock of rocks. Some of these reports at least are clearly established. In March 2015, a large group of snow geese passing through Idaho simply fell from the sky—more than two thousand of them, according to the Idaho Department of Fish and Game. A department spokesman, Gregg Losinski, was quoted as saying, "Basically, they just fell out of the sky." The agency formally suspected avian cholera was involved, and it quickly collected and burned the corpses to prevent any spread of the disease. If that was in fact the cause, it wasn't ever clearly established. And not everyone was convinced.

That was in March. Three months later, the residents of Kuna, southwest of Boise, were driving along their roadways only to encounter fallen, dead songbirds. Masses of them. No reliable numerical estimates were ever recorded, nor was a clear reason established why so many abruptly fell to the ground.

These things, at least, all really happened. They were established without dispute after sightings by many witnesses, and they were never refuted, even if their causes and surrounding stories remain unclear.

Idaho is full of many other mysteries too, things that may or may not be true, stories with many missing pieces or strange aspects or in which the details may be and could remain in heated dispute. And there are still other stories, more fanciful, that most people would not accept as strictly real, but these are stories where the exact bounds between reality and fantasy can be unclear. Or there are stories with legendary status, parts of ancient mythologies that some people still take on faith.

Some of them reach into primeval memory, deep into Idaho's prehistory. For example, in southwest Idaho the two most visually striking massive natural features, ranging high and sinking low, are located adjacent to each other: a mountain range and a canyon. The mountain range is called the Seven Devils; the gorge is called Hells Canyon. You may suspect coincidence was not at work in the naming of these features, and you would be right. And, oddly, the stories actually account for information that was not available when the stories were created, scientific data unearthed only with modern geology: that the mountains are relatively young in geologic age, and their contents include large deposits of copper.

The story traces to the Nez Perce bands roaming across and beyond the Blue Mountains northwest of Hells Canyon, and across the Snake River from the Seven Devils. It speaks of seven gigantic monsters residing in those mountains, monsters that made a practice of eating children. The Nez Perce children were said to be especially at risk, since they wandered near the same area—around the Blue Mountains, just west of Idaho—that the Nez Perce then did. (It sounds like a scary nighttime story parents might tell young children to encourage them not to run off, but it gained widespread currency anyway.)

The legend says the tribe's chiefs sought help from the supernatural figure known as Coyote. The problem was great enough that Coyote, who was sympathetic, in turn consulted with another supernatural figure, Fox, for additional counsel.

Fox developed a plan. He proposed that they dig seven holes—massive holes deep in the ground—in an area the seven giants frequented east of the Blue Mountains, and then cover them with boiling liquid. Digging animals like bears and beavers were employed to create the pits, and then a liquid described as looking like rust (this would match with the reference to copper) was poured into them. Fox and Coyote then heated a bunch of large rocks and threw them in, heating the liquid to near boiling.

When the giants walked through the area, they fell into the holes. Their splashing spread the rust-colored liquid all over the area, but their efforts to escape were to no avail. Coyote walked up to them and said, "You are being punished for your wickedness. I will punish you even more by changing you into seven mountains. I will make you very high so that everyone can see you. You will stand here forever, to remind people that your punishment comes from bad deeds. I will make a deep gash in the earth here so that no more of your family can get across to trouble my people."

The seven giants became the Seven Devils, and the gash in the earth became Hells Canyon.

Idaho is actually built on legends like that, stories that run large and run small.

The Owyhee Mountains, a hundred miles south of the Seven Devils, were said in ancient legends to be home to the "Owyhee dwarves" (the current version of that name was developed relatively recently). According to the stories, they were about two feet tall and had tails, which would switch behind them; they were wiry and strong. They were said to be eaters of people, notably of children.

Unfortunate things happening to children seems to be a recurring theme in very old Idaho legends. Travel east across the Snake River Plain, and you'll encounter another instance. About thirty miles west of Pocatello is a site where another grisly story relating to children was centered. The "water baby" story has been told in several places around the West, but it seems most associated with Idaho.

Today, the area where this story was set faces—or lies under—the American Falls Reservoir portion of the Snake River, backed up against the American Falls Dam north of I-86, and part of that area is in Massacre Rocks State Park. (You can tell already that a legend of some kind underlies that.)

The area once—from the 1500s into the 1700s—was dominated by bands of Shoshone Indians, who sometimes struggled to survive here since the area was desert, and water supplies, in the pre-reservoir days, were limited. At one point a famine hit so badly in the area that tribal members were dying from starvation.

The story says that some Shoshone mothers were driven to such desperation that after some of their babies were born, they would take them down to the stream—presumably the Snake River—and drown them, since they knew there would be no food for them.

But, the tale adds, that was not the end. The babies, or at least some of them, were said to survive in the water, developing gills and fins, living and even looking much like fish. They evolved into sprites and turned mean, attacking people who came their way—people like those who had dumped them into the water. They are still there, the story goes, sighing or calling out in an effort to attract people into the water.

In the generations since, Idaho has heard more tales of strange creatures. Bigfoot has been said to put in an appearance in Idaho from time to time, though the Gem State apparently hasn't been one of his favorite haunts. (Oregon and Montana seem to be more popular sighting places.) But there have been sightings. One of the most noted was a sighting of a mini-Bigfoot—the tracks were reported to be smaller than those usually noted for the creature—proclaimed around the mid-twentieth century by a group of eight people near the town of Lapwai in northern Idaho. But the details, even the date of the sighting, are sketchy.

That instance is far from solitary, however. Tales about Bigfoot have crisscrossed the state, as they have in many other places around the country. Idaho has had enough sightings that the Bigfoot Field Researchers Organization (yes, there is such a group, and it has a website) reported by the end of 2018 an accumulation of eighty-seven Bigfoot incidents in Idaho. The most striking and detailed account was by a camper in the Oakley area in July 1999; a similar sighting occurred eight years later near Hansen. The organization reports sightings in twenty-five of the state's forty-four counties (with a disproportionate sixteen sightings in Bonner County and thirteen in Valley County).

Many of the more recent myths and legends in Idaho, and many of those recounted in this book, have to do with hauntings, creatures, treasures, and strange places. Idaho seems to have no lack of any of them.

A photographer who lived in Idaho posted a story on his website describing one creepy haunted place somewhere in the eastern part of the state (he does not say exactly where, but there is some indication that it was in the Rexburg area). It consisted of an old abandoned cabin and the landscape around and under it. He said that in the story about the cabin, which dates to the early twentieth century, a man who was a college professor met and married an Indian woman. She was unhappy living in the city, so he moved far out of town, onto the plains, where he built a cabin for the two of them, and eventually their two children, to live in.

Over the years, for reasons unexplained, the professor went mad. He was said to have captured, collected, and trained wolves. He went crazier than that, finally, killing his family. Whether he was pursued is unknown, but the story said that neither he nor his wolves have been seen since. However, there are people who have claimed to visit the old cabin, and they have maintained that animal skins, some of relatively recent vintage, have been seen hanging there. There's also another coda to the story: Supposedly an underground tunnel was dug there, through which the professor may have escaped when police officers came after him.

The story adds that unusual sights and sounds have been observed in the area, and other odd events too. One person who reported having visited the place said in a blog post:

> I took the picture of that entrance (see Door to the Underworld) and it's pretty creepy. That door is right under the porch. Now, I've been to a few ghost towns, and believe very much in ghosts (I could tell more stories about myths in Idaho and my experiences if anyone wants) and this place didn't feel as bad as other places I've been to. But there was just one thing that was disconcerting, my friend was the one driving, and his car never randomly stops. When we got in front of the house, it kept turning off and he would have to restart it. This happened about 5 times, and he said when he went alone before that it happened a lot too.

More-conventional buildings are said to have been haunted as well.

Hauntings have been reported in at least two of Idaho's leading theaters. The Egyptian Theater, for generations a cultural jewel in Boise's downtown and one of the last remaining beautifully designed movie theaters in the region, is supposed to have haunted creatures lurking about. Something about the old Egyptian motif of the place seems to encourage the legend.

The Lewiston Civic Theater, which has a less distinctive look to it, is located in a building constructed in 1902 that was used as a

Methodist church until it was taken over by an arts group in 1971. About a decade later, three people—a man and two women—were reported to have vanished from the place without explanation. They were never seen again alive; the bodies of the women were recovered elsewhere in town, and no trace of the man was located. Since then, some Lewistonians have speculated that the building is haunted by the spirit of the man; alternatively, others claim to have spotted a female ghost wandering the stairs. Chandeliers and other fixtures are said to move about of their own volition.

In one case, a whole college campus was said to be haunted. That was the old "normal school" in Albion, in south-central Idaho. A teachers' college founded in 1892, it was one of Idaho's earlier colleges and expanded to become the Southern Idaho College of Education, but closed due to budget shortfalls in 1951. A counterpart school in Lewiston was later reopened, but, with a brief exception or two, the normal school stayed closed thereafter. (During one of its brief revivals it was called the Magic Christian College.) Its buildings were abandoned and their windows boarded.

They look like prospects for a good haunting.

Since then, visitors to the site have reported seeing ghosts and odd red eyes in the air and hearing voices. One family that owned the property in the new millennium permitted paranormal investigators to check out the area, and they reported odd occurrences there.

The Magic Valley has, true to its name, loads of instances of alleged hauntings.

Another institutional building located just outside Gooding, a former college building run by the Episcopal church and later a tuberculosis hospital operated by the state of Idaho, was long alleged to be haunted, with spirits wandering the floors.

Idaho's vast spaces, including enormous reaches of desert or forest or wilderness lands with no human habitation at all, are home to many creatures. Many of them are well known, and some have hunting or fishing permits attached to their harvest. Stories have emerged about other sorts of creatures as well.

Some are simply a joke; near the Yellowstone National Park area (Idaho claims a slice of that park), postcards and souvenirs featuring the legendary "jackalope" have been reliable sellers for a long time.

The most striking creature sightings in Idaho have been of another sort altogether. There are the sightings of creatures in bodies of water, including the "Paddler" of Lake Pend Oreille and "Sharlie" of Payette Lake. You'll see a longer review later in this book of the many sightings of still another, the Bear Lake Monster. Idaho also has been home, in two locations (outside Orofino and outside Lava Hot Springs), to a semilegendary tale of a group of creatures that definitely are real: ligers, which are crossbred lions and tigers. They were brought to Idaho (from Oregon) by enthusiasts in 1986. About a decade later, some of them escaped from a compound outside Lava Hot Springs, and reports of the ligers and their recapture went viral through international news reports. Some people in the area wonder if a few of the creatures might still be wandering the hills.

They certainly are not forgotten. About thirty miles away from Lava Hot Springs is the small farming town of Preston, the thinly disguised setting for the comedy movie *Napoleon Dynamite*. Several animals show up in the course of the film, but the title character says that none of them is his favorite animal. That, he said, is the liger.

There are other sorts of legends. As a part of Old West territory, and for that matter part of its crossroads, Idaho was a hot spot for treasures, buried and otherwise.

There were robberies of various kinds around Idaho Territory, some involving amounts of gold and other valuables considered big stakes for the time. At least one Idaho sheriff was involved in one case. Another treasure was thought to be hidden behind an iron door half buried in the mountains—a door that itself seems to have vanished.

Idaho has its selection too of strange places. In the middle of Idaho's hottest deserts, on the edge of territory once covered by molten lava fields, you can find (it's actually a significant tourist attraction) a massive ice cave with some of the strangest properties to be found anywhere in the state—and which, depending on whom you talk to, also may be haunted. There are rumors, going back more than a century, of a massive tunnel system underlying the Boise city downtown; though many historians say the tunnels never existed, they have never exactly been disproved either. There is a lake in northern Idaho that exhibits some weird properties, enough to give it the name Spirit Lake, and seems to have exported some of those properties to the town on its shore.

Finally, there is this question: What is real? What's a strange but true fact, and what's just a good story? The lines have been hard to draw in some cases. There is—or was (it's demolished now)—a house that is said to have been occupied by the mistress of, and with the assistance of, a president of the United States. Supposedly Butch Cassidy robbed a bank in Idaho, and the story has become a foundation of local lore; but was it him, or might it have been someone else?

Idaho really is a legendary kind of place, after its fashion.

There's a lot of empty space here, psychic as well as physical, yet to be filled in.

CHAPTER 1

Chinese Tunnels

Boise had a Chinatown; that much is undisputed, and it was substantial enough that news stories about it once spread around the western states. It extended, at its peak, across about a half-dozen blocks on the southern side of the downtown area, its northern boundary running a couple of blocks south of the state capitol building. It included an array of commercial buildings, some cramped residential areas, and service businesses.

Many stories and rumors surrounded the old Chinatown area, but the most persistent is this: Are there actual tunnels built by Chinese residents of the downtown area buried underneath central Boise? If there were, what were they used for, and where did they lead?

You can find around Boise a significant number of people who will swear that there are, or at least were, tunnels in this area. Others, including local historians and city officials who have looked into the city's underground and studied maps, building diagrams, and engineering reports, are equally determined that there are not.

The question has recurred over the decades and has not gone away, even very recently.

In July 2017, researchers organizing old files in the Idaho State Archives were working inside a climate-controlled vault, through material sitting there for decades, when they ran across an obscure piece of film footage, a remnant from the early days of local Boise television. About fifteen minutes long, it was extremely fragile. The archivists had an old film projector of the type used in the 1960s, when the film was shot, but they calculated that running it through the projector would destroy it. They decided to try digitizing it instead.

It went on a long list of digitizing projects, and finally emerged from that process in April 2018. The bad news was that no sound remained, and much of what the film had to say was lost with the missing audio.

The visuals were there, however, and they immediately got researchers' attention. When in May the video went public and aired on local television news programs, viewers were startled.

The film showed a news report from 1967, created at Boise television station KBOI (later renamed KBSI, and now KBOI once again). The reporter was named Sam Donaldson (not the national television personality), a veteran Boise reporter who wore "Buddy Holly glasses" (as one newspaper article described them) and later went on to work for Boise Cascade Corporation. He was standing in what then remained of downtown Boise's Chinatown, at the old Hip Sing Association building.

The video then showed him talking with several people, veterans of the Chinatown area. One was Raymond Fong, whose family had worked in the district for several generations. Another interviewee was the now-elderly son of a former Boise police chief. The son seemed to be the main source—in the footage remaining—for the historical background in the report.

When the tape aired, it got a response from Idaho Public Television, where a producer said she had been able to locate a short piece of the report—about six minutes—still available in records there, this one including sound. When this material was played, however, it didn't add much information; it contained clips chopped up and intended for use in a 1990 state centennial document. There were few complete sentences and little identification of key figures.

The news report seemed to have been prompted by the impending sale of the Hip Sing building, and whatever lay in the ground below it. Donaldson was pointing to a hole in the pavement, a place where a bunch of pipes were strewn about. Then he said, "In this coal room was the start of the Chinese tunnels. In fact, the start was right here, at this concrete patch. The patch is here today, but the tunnels are gone. Or at least they're gone for the most part." He then showed a small map of downtown that included dotted lines where the tunnels were supposed to have been.

David Matte, administrator of the state archives, told the *Idaho Statesman* newspaper, "I found the piece a very interesting part of the debate of whether there were or were not Chinese tunnels in Boise at one time. It's not proof enough for me to be persuaded completely, but I would not rule out the possibility if new evidence was ever gathered and verified."

Some historians were not convinced at all. Arthur Hart, a longtime historian at the Idaho Historical Society, wrote a book about Boise's Chinatown, and he has flatly dismissed the idea. Hart described the tunnels as nothing more than "legend."

Others begged to differ. The *Statesman* also talked with Dottie Robinson, a daughter-in-law of the police chief's son, who said her relatives had told her detailed stories of walking through the old tunnels. "Arthur Hart has never believed those tunnels were there ... BUT THEY WERE," she said in an e-mail. "Don't mean to bore you, but I get tired of defending the 'tunnels.'"

The earliest settlements in Idaho were set up as mining camps—first in Pierce City, in north-central Idaho; the year after in Florence, about a hundred miles south of Pierce; and the year following in Idaho City, in the mountains northeast of what is now Boise. Soon after the camps' development, miners and providers of goods and services showed up, many of them coming from the sloweddown mines in northern California. A significant number of the new arrivals in these mining and mine service communities were Chinese.

One small group from California, who were said to have originated mainly from the Guangdong Province in China, passed through the even newer town of Boise in 1864, and trekked up into the mountains to the area called the Boise, centered on Idaho City. A much larger group arrived the following year. To their numbers were added a significant number of Asian workers of various origins on the Union Pacific railroad line, which was being built across southern Idaho in the 1880s. Their numbers grew rapidly, and by 1870 the census reported that they accounted for 45 percent of the population in Idaho City.

After the boom of the 1860s, Idaho City largely went bust in the 1870s, however, and all sectors of Idaho City's population slid. Many of the people there moved downhill to Boise, which was growing rapidly. The Chinese residents, who worked in a variety of service trades and owned a number of local businesses, were among them, and many congregated in part of the downtown area. The area centered on either side of Main Street from about 6th Street to 9th Street—in all, about a half-dozen blocks, though the exact size and configuration are open to debate.

As in many other cities in the West, the area was referred to as Chinatown. In Boise, the area was active enough that it was considered to have had two distinct phases of development, in the 1870s and 1880s, called the first and second Chinatowns. Many of the buildings there had a distinctive look and style that marked them for the region.

A wide variety of businesses and other activities flourished there, serving not only the ethnic but also the broader regional population, most of them legitimate, a few not, dealing in illicit goods and activities. Some cultural artifacts crossed the Pacific, and while one long-running store specialized in herbal medicines, other products and services could be had too. These included opium.

There was some irony to this. Chinese emperors long had sought to ban or suppress the use of opium in their country and in the early 1800s declared, "Opium has a harm. Opium is a poison, undermining our good customs and morality. Its use is prohibited by law." The country fought, unsuccessfully, two "opium wars" in the 1840s and 1850s with Great Britain—which wanted to pursue a trade in the substance—and was never quite able to stamp it out. British prime minister William Ewart Gladstone decried the second of these conflicts as "a war more unjust in its origin, a war more

A Chinese New Year celebration in Boise's old Chinatown area, allegedly the site of an underground tunnel system.
IDAHO STATE HISTORICAL SOCIETY

calculated in its progress to cover this country with permanent disgrace." He was joined in that opinion by many others in both Britain and the United States.

But Britain was not the only trader in opium in those years; a number of American businessmen, including renowned merchant John Jacob Astor, engaged in it as well. In a drug trade remarkable in its day for global reach, he sold Turkish opium in China to obtain a number of other products from that country. The opium originally came from many places—including Chinese manufacturers—and traveled to many as well.

Opium remained a significant export item from China well into the twentieth century, and when large numbers of Chinese workers came to the western United States in the second half of the nineteenth century, the trade came along with them.

Opium was popular in the United States, and long had been. More than a quarter millennium before America's recent opioid epidemic, Benjamin Franklin used it as a painkiller in his later years. Its use exploded in the mid-1800s with two developments: the introduction of the hypodermic syringe just before the Civil War, and the immense and massive treatment of wounded soldiers during the conflict. Over the next couple of decades, use of it spread widely, becoming a true precursor to—and possibly even larger in scope than—the opioid crisis of the new millennium. How broadly its use expanded was noted in the estimate that more than half, and possibly 60 percent, of all American users in the latter 1800s were women. Generally, all of this for many years was legal.

Writing in the *Smithsonian* magazine, Erick Trickey noted:

Opium smoking spread across the United States from the 1870s into the 1910s, with Chinese immigrants operating opium dens in most major cities and Western towns. They attracted both indentured Chinese immigrant workers and white Americans, especially "lower-class urban males, often neophyte members of the underworld," according to *Dark Paradise* [a book about opium addiction in America]. "It's a poor town now-a-days that has not a Chinese laundry," a white opium-smoker said in 1883, "and nearly every one of these has its layout"—an opium pipe and accessories. That shift created a political opening for prohibition.

That legal pushback, which was coupled with anti-Chinese bigotry, came relatively early in Idaho. There was little political resistance to it because clamping down on people from across the Pacific was a core component of Idaho policy and politics in territorial days—alongside, in those days, harassment of Mormons—and openly engaged in at the legislative level. From statehood until 1962 the Idaho Constitution banned people of Asian ancestry from serving on juries, voting, or holding elective office.

An early Idaho territorial legislature—one estimate put the date at 1879, though the records are unclear on the timing—passed a measure aimed at cracking down on the opium trade, an indication that that form of commerce had become substantial enough by then to draw the attention of local authorities. The measure set fines for "keeping of places of resort for smoking opium or frequenting same." Boise police used the new law to raid various places in and around Chinatown, and Boise city soon added more ordinances of its own.

The law enforcement crackdown continued over several decades. In 1895, federal law enforcement officials came to Boise to raid opium dens still in existence, and concluded that large amounts of opium were run through the city. One source put the amount at a thousand pounds a month. The *Idaho Statesman* concluded, "This city does seem to be a general supply point for this entire portion of the state."

All of this clearly had the effect of driving the trade in opium—and, by some reports, prostitution as well—underground, probably literally so. Veteran Boise writer Dwight Jensen said in his book *Visiting Boise* that while Chinatown probably had no extended tunnels, "there were underground opium dens from which the tunnel stories probably originated."

The prostitution element too probably existed to a limited degree, but may have been small in scale if it existed at all, because Boise at that time already had its own separate red-light district, just east of the Chinatown area, and it would not be closed down by city officials until around the turn of the twentieth century.

In his book about Boise's Chinatown, Hart reported:

Workmen repairing Eighth Street between Main and Idaho in June 1898 uncovered a large hole in front of the Odd Fellows Hall. It was the paper's opinion that it was an underground opium den from the city's early days when the area was part of Chinatown. A white man called "Chinese Anthony", because of his association with the Chinese, had owned the adjoining property. This, and earlier incidents, as when a team of horses fell through rotting planks into a series of excavations behind Chinese buildings on Idaho Street in 1888, contributed to the legend repeated to this day, that the city is honeycombed with Chinese tunnels.

There's little doubt that some underground activity was underway in the Chinatown area in the late 1800s. Boise did not have a true city water supply system until the 1900s. It had no sewer system either until 1892, and before that, cesspools were dug by many businesses in the area, not only Chinese, for disposal; in Chinatown, those diggings were used for laundry runoff as well. Full-length tunnels, of the sort running entire blocks or more, have never been located in the area, however.

In the 1960s, the city of Boise, eager to revitalize its downtown area, launched a massive urban redevelopment effort. The first major effect, and for a couple of decades its largest one, was the demolition of a large piece of downtown ("downtown urban removal," it was called), including nearly all of the old Chinatown district, except for three or four buildings at its fringe. The effort also wiped out much of Boise's physical history and outraged more than a few residents. Writer L. J. Davis, who grew up in Boise, wrote in 1974 in an article for *Harper's Magazine*, "If things go on as they are, Boise stands an excellent chance of becoming the first American city to have deliberately eradicated itself." Not much of Chinatown, on the ground level or below it, was left to explore after that.

As Hart has pointed out, most of old Chinatown was so thoroughly demolished and even many underground areas ripped up in the Boise urban redevelopment efforts of the late 1960s and early 1970s that any extensive tunnel system would have been uncovered—presumably. Small storage rooms and old cesspool facilities were found, but no long tunnels were seen by the construction crews.

Hart concluded in his book, "Tacoma, Pendleton, Nampa and other Northwest cities have similar legends, but they have no tunnels either. Like all urban tales, this one is too intriguing not to be repeated whether it is true or not."

It continues to be repeated, and the search for the tunnels goes on.

There do exist, however, a little-known set of tunnels underneath another major Idaho city, a much larger system of underground channels than anything imagined for Boise. And their presence is not in any dispute, though the people who manage them usually have avoided publicity concerning them, and they are not nearly as often publicly discussed.

These are the Rock Creek Canyon tunnels, close by the city of Twin Falls and edging toward its south and east. The main entryway, called the Klaar Tunnel, was built about a century ago, but its origins are far more prosaic than the questionable tunnels of Boise. These tunnels—there were about fifty altogether—were part of the project to bring irrigation water to the Magic Valley.

The Magic Valley in south-central Idaho is so named because of human efforts, many of them engineered through the U.S. Bureau of Reclamation and a number of local agencies, that turned forbidding desert into verdant cropland. Dam construction was an important part of that, and the 1905 development of the Milner Dam on the Snake River, east of Twin Falls, was a centerpiece. Water banked from it was spread out to new irrigators for miles around.

Controlling the water proved difficult. Like much of southern Idaho, a great deal of the thin soil around Twin Falls sat atop a thick bed of basalt rock, spread there from the massive lava eruptions centered around what is now the Craters of the Moon National Monument. The water often did not sink properly into the soil, but ran off. The water table was hard to control.

Brian Olmstead, a veteran manager of the Twin Falls Canal Company, was quoted by the *Twin Falls Times News*, "They tried everything to bring down the water table after Milner (dam) was built. They dug tile drainages and drilled wells, but what they found was that by digging tunnels 30 to 40 feet below the surface, they could drain some of that water from the top and bottom." By carefully drilling through the twisting rock formations, they were able to reach the Rock Creek Canyon and divert some of the water there.

The project turned out to be immensely complex. The core of it started in 1926 with equipment trucked in from Montana, along with fifty pounds of dynamite. About seventy-five men were involved in working that early effort, a number that eventually grew to more than three hundred fifty. Some of them died during the occasionally hazardous work, which lasted a quarter century until 1951. About fifty tunnels, crisscrossing an area the size of a small town, were blasted through the rock. It was one of the largest construction projects southern Idaho has ever seen—or rather, has never seen, since it was invisible to most of the people in the area.

While the tunnels were developed primarily for water management and were never intended to be publicly accessible, some people found alternative uses for some of the chambers. In the early years, during Prohibition, bootleggers were reported to have used them both for storage and to locate distilleries, until law enforcement caught on and wiped out those operations. Later, and because the temperature of the tunnels stayed at a near-constant level in the mid-50s, homeless people sometimes used the tunnels for shelter in the winter. The Klaar and many of the other tunnels are physically large enough to support such activities. Many are about six feet tall and four or five feet wide. Water often continues to run on the floors, but typically does not engulf the tunnels.

Some of them were lengthy. The longest was said to be the Orchalara Tunnel, which runs roughly east-west along what is now the southern edge of Twin Falls. Like many of the other tunnels, it has been sealed, or at least blocked from public access, and the access points are obscure even to longtime residents of the area. In Idaho, even the official tunnels sometimes remain the subject of mystery and curiosity.

CHAPTER 2

Wetxuwiis

The first half of September 1805 was a hard-traveling time for the expedition led by Captains Meriwether Lewis and William Clark. The Corps of Discovery was well into its second year of travel, but the experience wasn't making travel easier. Stress was growing.

The expedition had been on the move since May 14, 1804, when they took off from Camp Dubois, near the confluence of the Missouri and Mississippi Rivers. The Corps was headed west to at least the reaches of the Louisiana Purchase territory, which ran through the Missouri River basin, and intended to go even farther, all the way to the Pacific Ocean. President Thomas Jefferson wanted something better than speculation and rumor; he wanted to know what really was out there. It mattered, because without hard information the westward growth of the new United States would be stunted.

The summer months were not difficult for the crew; they were, after all, accustomed to traveling through wilderness territory, since so much of the United States east of the Mississippi was undeveloped. Contacts with native tribes went peacefully, for the most part, but sometimes tensely; at one point in September, a band of the Lakota Sioux demanded one of their boats as a toll, in effect, for continuing on. But they managed with only one casualty, Sergeant Charles Floyd, who died of a ruptured appendix. The group stopped in November to winter at their own construction of Fort Mandan, in what is now North Dakota, not one of the easiest places along their route for settling for the winter, but they survived there.

The Corps of Discovery left Fort Mandan, headed west the following April, and trudged across the vast spaces of what is now Montana. They made steady progress, but more than a year of travel finally was beginning to take its toll. Supplies grew tighter, food progressively harder to find (or catch), and illnesses more frequent.

August was a time of transition, the opening of a critical period. Lewis and Clark both had birthdays that month, but more important was the new barrier they had just encountered, and apparently had not expected. The Continental Divide was just ahead, along with the most challenging mountains, by far, they had yet seen. In mid-August, they met with a band of Shoshone who sold them horses and supplies for the climb ahead, but they seem to have overestimated their physical capacity for the mountain climb. Later in the month, they crossed the Continental Divide at Lemhi Pass, out of the Missouri River basin, and left behind what was considered U.S. territory.

They now were moving into the disputed Oregon lands, which for decades would be contested by the United States and Great Britain. Up to this point they had the advantage of intelligence from wandering hunters and often-friendly natives who had previously had occasional contact with at least a few people from the United States. The landscape they were entering now was, in comparison, a complete blank, unknown territory. They knew nothing of what lay on the other side of those mountains. Communications even among the tribes on the opposing sides of the mountains were more occasional than they were ordinary.

The trip over the high and jagged Bitterroot Mountains did not go easily. Several of their horses died, with scant evident opportunity to replace them, though the expedition did buy thirteen more from a Flathead band it encountered. By the time they made their way downhill through an early snow on the west side of the pass, food began to run out. By mid-September the travelers were beginning to starve, reduced to eating even candles—and some of the horses. They were sick, and seemed to be getting worse.

The Corps hiked, slowly, on the Lolo Trail, a pathway first set by the native bands who lived mainly to the west—natives whom they were, unaware, approaching.

By September 20 they had reached a flat and open area, now called the Weippe Plain. Lewis was sick enough that he stayed close by the camp, taking notes about several new species of birds he had seen. Clark—feeling none too well himself—headed west with a scouting party to see what lay ahead. What lay ahead was a close call Lewis and Clark never fully appreciated, involving a native people unlike any they had seen before.

The people who were just around the bend were an indigenous band most commonly called, among outsiders, the Nez Perce tribe. The tribe ordinarily uses the name Niimíipuu in its self-descriptions, and that word shows up on many buildings and locations in the present-day reservation. A tribe member named Otis Halfmoon, recounting the tribe's history, said:

We also call ourselves Tsoopnitpeloo, and Tsoopnitpeloo means "The Walking-Out People"—people from the mountains come to the plains, to hunt buffalo. And that was our old-time name. A long time ago, how these people communicate, was through sign language. And our sign was, accordingly, was the right finger out, and a downward motion in front of the face, to show, from the mountains, come to the plains to hunt buffalo. And somewhere along the way a French fur trapper, and some other tribes as well, thought that meant "pierced nose." But we never pierced our nose. Nez Perce was a French word that does mean "pierced nose," but we never did that.

A native interpreter (who didn't know them well) called them the *Chupnit-pa-lu*, which Clark would translate loosely into "Chopunnish." That is the name the Corps would give—in the form of Camp Chopunnish—to the fort they would use as a base on their return journey, not far from where they first encountered the people.

The Niimíipuu were a major economic and military force in the Pacific Northwest, and the most populous group in the region. Their ancestral territory cut across what is now north-central Idaho, northeastern Oregon, and the far southeastern slice of Washington, spread across about a hundred villages, split among more than a dozen bands. Their hunting and gathering spanned the region from the Cascade Mountains in the west to the Bitterroot Mountains in the east.

It went even farther than that. At some points in the mid-1700s the Niimíipuu reached out to the east side of the Bitterroots and made a friendly economic, social, and eventually military alliance with the Salish people living there. The Salish had a long-standing rivalry with the Blackfeet, who lived not far away, and eventually joined in conflicts with the Blackfeet. Later, in the late 1700s, they withdrew back to the west side of the mountains, but not before they suffered casualties—including the kidnapping of some of their tribal members.

The Niimíipuu had experience and communications with native tribes across the West, but not much with the lighter-skinned strangers from the East. There was, however, an eerie prophecy well known among the bands. The prophecy songs of the Niimíipuu went back many years, but they seemed remarkably on point in 1805. They had never seen a European—a white-skinned person—but the prophecy songs seemed to foretell of them, of another race of people who would divide the land that had always been indivisible, that the earth and even the sky would change—and not in good ways. Now, in the small, open Weippe Prairie, in the mountains above the Clearwater River, William Clark and the three or four fellow travelers with him probably were the first people from what is now the United States ever to stand before them. They had some cause, actually an array of causes, to be wary of strangers. And now a group of strangers, with more of them camped in the woods not far away, had appeared in their midst.

Clark, recovering from illness and leading a group in desperate need of food, had taken a hunting party of six forward from the Corps' main camp to scout ahead for something to eat. They were spotted by three boys from one of the tribal villages. The boys tried

The rugged Bitterroot Mountains, through which Lewis and Clark hiked on their way to meeting the Nez Perce.

hiding from the party at first, but Clark offered them ribbons as gifts, to signal good intentions.

That was about as much as they could communicate. Lewis and Clark had added to their crew a few interpreters from tribes along the way, and in many cases, languages were closely enough related that neighboring or even distant tribes could communicate with interpreters from far away. The Nez Perce language, however, separated as it was by the Bitterroot Mountains from that of groups previously encountered, was different enough that comprehension of words was nearly impossible. A rough form of sign language was as much as they were able to accomplish.

News of the arrival of the strangers flew through the nearby villages, and discussion quickly ensued about what should be done next.

The leading figure there at the time was a chief named Walam-mottinin (literally "Hair Bunched and Tied"), soon to be known by the explorers as Twisted Hair. The Nez Perce were an egalitarian people, and while Twisted Hair's impulses appear to have run to generosity, not everyone felt that way. Tales had circulated about what happened farther east when natives and white intruders met, and natives usually did not fare well. The long-standing tradition among the Niimíipuu was that a substantial portion were in favor of eliminating the threat.

They could easily have done that. The Lewis and Clark party was tired, sick, hungry, more or less lost, and in no condition to defend itself. Without outside help, their chances of getting as far as the Pacific Ocean, which they had no idea how to reach, were less than even.

They looked strange, in many ways. And the white men were not even the aspect of the group that caused the most unease. Their number included a few natives of the Shoshone bands, people little known from the far side of the Bitterroots but whose intentions were unclear. There were more specific concerns: Some of the Niimíipuu warriors were at that time off battling Shoshone warriors.

Allen V. Pinkham, coauthor of a book about Lewis and Clark's encounters with the Niimíipuu (*Lewis and Clark among the Nez Perce*), remarked that had the warrior contingent been at full strength, "there would have been more debate about should we kill them or not. A map we found showed an ambush site at Weippe. They had things we needed and wanted. It would make our lives easier. What would happen if we killed them all? We knew that east of the Mississippi there were tens upon tens of thousands of these same kinds of creatures."

Memories of what had happened with the Blackfeet were still clear in those minds; what were these other people up to?

Instead, the natives chose a different course.

When the following day arrived, the Niimíipuu welcomed the straggling Corps of Discovery into their camp. An anthropologist named Alice Fletcher in 1889 retold the stories, told by both Clark on one side and the villagers on the other, that the natives "were kind to the tired and hungry party. They furnished fresh horses and dried meat and fish with wild potatoes and other roots which were good to eat, and the refreshed white men went further on, westward, leaving their bony, worn-out horses for the Indians to take care of and have fat and strong when Lewis and Clark should come back on their way home."

The Niimíipuu were intrigued by elements of what the explorers brought with them: the guns, for one. They also took note of the religion they espoused, and were interested enough in it that years later they would send explorers of their own to white settlements to learn more. The first long-running Christian missionary operations in the Northwest would be set up, decades later, in Niimíipuu territory.

They provided guides for Lewis and Clark, and gave them explicit directions for heading out toward the Pacific coast. They helped them build canoes and other craft, and took them to their Canoe Camp, at what is now the city of Orofino, where they put in to the Clearwater River. From there, another forty miles or so downstream, they would encounter the Snake River; after many more miles of mostly easy travel on it, the Snake would pour into the Columbia, which ran all the way to the Pacific. The trip would not be as easy as the description may have made it sound, and there were mishaps within a few miles of the start on the Clearwater, but the Niimíipuu knew their way around the West, and the course—which the expedition followed—was accurate.

When Lewis and Clark returned east from the Pacific, they stopped again at the camp near the Clearwater, and found once again the helpful hospitality they had experienced before. In May and June of 1806, the Corps built a camp and rested at what they called Camp Chopunnish, not far from present-day Lapwai, where they gathered food and supplies and otherwise prepared for what they knew would be a difficult crossing back over the Bitterroots. Except that, with help from the Niimíipuu, it was less difficult this time than it was the year before—in part because the tribe gave the explorers advice on when to travel (advice ignored at first, then adopted when the weather turned bad).

The mystery in all this is why the Niimíipuu were so especially friendly to the expedition. They may have been the single most helpful group of Native Americans anywhere along the tremendous distance Lewis and Clark covered. No minutes were kept of the Niimíipuu deliberations, so no firm written record remains showing how the tribe decided to deal with the explorers.

But there are oral traditions, and they are consistent. They center on a woman named Wetxuwiis (or, in other writings, Wat-ku-ese), a member of the tribe who is said to have made the argument fiercely and passionately that the travelers should be helped.

An early annotator of the Lewis and Clark journals, Reuben Gold Thwaites, reported:

There is a tradition among the Nez Perce Indians that when Lewis and Clark first visited the Chopunnish, the latter were inclined to kill the white men—a catastrophe which was averted by the influence of a woman in that tribe. She had been captured by hostile Indians, and carried into Manitoba, where some white people enabled her to escape; and finally, she returned to her own tribe. . . . Hearing her people talk of killing the explorers, she urged them to do no harm to the white men, but to treat them with kindness and hospitality—counsel which they followed.

Otis Halfmoon offered a more detailed description of the background of Wat-ku-ese.

He said that she had been a girl traveling with the Niimíipuu bands who camped with the Salish, on the east side of the Bitterroot Mountains, decades before, and had been there when the Blackfeet attacked. She was captured by them and enslaved, turned into commercial trading property. She was said to have been traded to the Cree Tribe, farther east, and then to the Chippewa, even farther east—by now almost halfway across the continent from her home lands.

Then—she is said to have reported—she was purchased by a white family, probably somewhere in the Great Lakes region, and was treated well by its members. They in turn were traveling west, and decided that she should be allowed to return home to her own people. In a long-running journey as remarkable as that of Lewis and Clark, she was handed off to the Mandan people at their major trading center in what are now the Dakotas—not far from where Lewis and Clark would hunker down for their first winter. And then she is said to have made her way to the Crow people, then to the Salish, and finally back across the Bitterroots to the Niimíipuu.

The name Wat-ku-ese is said to mean "Lost and Then Was Found."

Halfmoon continued:

> She told about a race of people was as numerous as the leaves in the trees. There was so many of them, so powerful, and they had all these wonderful things that they had, and so many beautiful things. And that these people would eventually come to our people, some day. Well, she came back, and she told those stories, and no one would believe her. They thought she was crazy. They thought somebody had hit her in the head really hard, or something because, man, they never heard of these things before. And all of a sudden, in 1805, here we find Lewis and Clark coming out of the mountains. And also one man is completely black.

He said her message was, "Now, now is the time. It is these white people. Help 'em. Do what you can. Feed 'em. Because it was these people here that helped me when I was a slave. When all the other Indian people treated me so bad, these people were the ones treated me well. Feed 'em. Do what you can."

Did it happen? Did the strong advocacy of one woman save the Lewis and Clark expedition, and in so doing shape the larger history of the American West? We can't be sure, but it seems more likely than not. In his September 21 journal entry, Clark said that in the village led by Twisted Hair lived a woman who "had formerly been taken by the Minitarries of the north & Seen white men," and had been friendly toward them.

In 2003, a regional historian, Zoa L. Swayne, wrote a somewhat fictionalized but carefully researched book called *Do Them No Harm! Lewis and Clark among the Nez Perce*. As she tells the story, Wetxuwiis heard talk among some of the other villagers, uneasy about the strange newcomers, and said, "Men like these were good to me. Do not kill them. Do them no harm!"

Swayne later wrote that "through the years the author has heard the story of Wat-ku-ese from many Nez Perces: Mary Kipp, Richard Moffett, Beatrice Miles, Harry Wheeler. The stories have been essentially the same, but with slight variations."

The stories are similar enough that other researchers have said that this legend—as it clearly also is a legend—probably is at least generally true.

CHAPTER 3

The Monster of Bear Lake

The Bear Lake Monster
Climb a tree, quick, here comes the Bear Lake Monster;
With Joseph C. Rich astride, acting as sponsor.
Hide in the branches well, and all stop breathing;
Finding no boys to eat, soon they'll be leaving.

Hush, through the brush they rush, all decked in sage and yellow.
Just see the horses run, just hear the cattle bellow.
Oh Joe, you cruel fo—good riddance to the sponsor;
Just hear them blow, there they go, good-bye, you horrid monster.

—AN OLD FOLK SONG WRITTEN AND

CHANTED IN THE BEAR LAKE AREA

Northern Idaho, and the mountains of central Idaho, are home to some of the most spectacular lakes to be found anywhere in the western United States. Southern Idaho is relatively dry land with fewer large bodies of water, many of those placid man-made reservoirs, and it has fewer lakes overall to offer—but it does have one of the largest, and one of the most remarkable.

With all of the larger lakes around Idaho come stories of lake monsters. Idaho is not alone in this. Most other states have their lake monsters too. Just across the border to the west, to cite one example, there's the tale of the Wallowa Lake monster in Oregon. But all of Idaho's larger lakes are notably well stocked with strange, and likely mythical, creatures.

From Payette Lake in Valley County, at McCall, comes the story of Sharlie.

Supposedly, Native Americans living in the area tried to warn off white settlers by talking about an evil spirit in the lake. But regular and consistent stories about Sharlie actually started later, around 1920, when loggers working near the lake said they thought they saw a "log" moving all by itself. Maybe it really was just a log (the city of McCall, which is on the lakeshore, got its start as a mill town). Regardless, a legend was born.

In 1944 and again in 1946, several groups of people claimed in unison to have seen the monster. One of them, a Nampa resident named G. A. Taylor, said, "It appeared to be between 30 and 40 feet long and seemed to keep diving into the water. It left a wake about like a small motor boat would make." More-specific descriptions of exactly what it looked like proved elusive.

More supposed sightings followed, one of them as recent as 2002, but Sharlie soon became more a lever for local tourism promotion than anything else. That effort goes back more than half a century. In 1954, the McCall newspaper, the *Star-News*, held a contest to name the monster, which until then had been short of a moniker. (The native tribes had spoken only of a spirit.) One reader replied, "Why don't you call the thing Sharlie? You know—'Vas you dere, Sharlie?'" That was a takeoff on a catchphrase used in a popular radio talk show of the day; Sharlie was a reference to "Charley."

The name stuck, even as the credibility of the sightings suffered.

From the north in Idaho's panhandle come stories of a fish-woman—no, it doesn't get a lot clearer than that—living in the depths of Lake Coeur d'Alene, somewhere close to a pointed rock. It is said to live with a giant underwater horned monster known (or at least said) to have lifted boats up from underneath.

And not far north of that, in the larger Lake Pend Oreille, comes the story of the "Paddler," said to be large and gray and speculated by some locals to be a remnant from the Jurassic era. Debunkers suggest it's actually just one of the submarines that were stationed periodically at the old World War II–era Farragut Naval Training Station on the eastern side of the lake.

The best known of Idaho's lake monsters is not known ordinarily by any specific name. It's just called the "Monster."

By far the largest lake in southern Idaho (at about 109 square miles) is Bear Lake, in the far southeastern corner of the state. It is the major standing water body in the Bear River system, which sprawls across Idaho, Utah, and Wyoming; Bear Lake itself is split between Idaho and Utah. Bear is a freshwater lake, and a significant vacation spot around the Cache Mountains region. (Just the Utah portion makes it the second-largest freshwater lake in that state; many lakes in northern Utah are, in contrast, salty.)

It has an unusual look, a turquoise coloration caused by a calcium carbonate deposit and buildup. It is a relatively old lake, about a quarter-million years old in something like its current configuration.

Why it is called "Bear Lake" is unclear, other than that someone must have spotted a bear in the area sometime long ago; the
explorer and fur trader Donald McKenzie is said to have called it
Black Bear Lake, which is at least a little more specific. The area
around Bear Lake is in the Idaho range of the American black bear,
and the creatures have been observed not far away.

Aside from the Native American tribes, mainly the Shoshone,
passing through the area, the earliest visitors here seem to have been
French-Canadian trappers, who traveled the Bear River basin in
around 1820 and held rendezvous there later in the decade. The lake
was known to mapmakers, but oddly, it was bypassed when the major
national trails—like the Oregon Trail—were being blazed west.

Although it is a freshwater lake, few people expressed much
interest in settling it until the 1860s. At that point, leaders of the
Church of Jesus Christ of Latter-Day Saints, reacting to the population concentration in the Salt Lake Valley, were pushing for creating new farming settlements, mainly toward more-verdant points
north. One of those settlements led to the founding of the first
Idaho town, at Franklin, just north of the Utah line. (The disputed
story goes that those settlers thought they still were on the Utah
side of the line.) Soon after that, church leader Brigham Young
asked an established and respected leader in the Salt Lake valley,
Charles Rich, to found another settlement to the northeast, around
Bear Lake. Rich gathered people and supplies and did that, starting
in 1863, and the settlement soon grew. A string of communities
sprouted to the west and north sides of the lake, mainly on what is
now the Idaho part of the lake.

Before very long, the newcomers and their friends back in Salt Lake City started to hear about the Bear Lake Monster.

Before setting up settlements around Bear Lake, the Mormon settlers met with local native tribes for clearance to move in. As with any longtime occupant, they passed along what they knew of the place, including tales of a monster in the lake. One native legend, related in 1874 to a traveler named John Goodman, told of two illicit lovers in the valley who were chased to the lake by fellow tribesmen. The Great Spirit took sympathy on them and, when they reached the water, transformed them into two giant serpents.

That was only one of the many stories told about the monster, and the variety of stories led to a multiplicity of descriptions of what it looked like. Here is one recent compilation from the Bear Lake Rendezvous Chamber of Commerce:

A creature with a brown-colored body, somewhat bigger in circumference than a man, anywhere from 40 to 200 feet long. Its head was shaped like a walrus without tusks or like an alligator's, and the eyes were very large and about a foot apart. It had ears like bunches, about the size of a pint cup. It had an unknown number of legs, approximately eighteen inches long, and it was awkward on land, but swam with a serpent-like motion at a speed of at least sixty miles an hour. No one ever described the back part of the animal since the head and forepart was all that was ever seen. The rest was always under water.

That might suggest a tale dreamed up as a tourist stunt (and the local chambers seem never to have minded making use of it), but the stories go back much further. In 1868, Joseph C. Rich, the founder and pillar of the Bear Lake community, sent a description of what he had heard to the *Deseret News*, the newspaper in Salt Lake City:

The Indians have a tradition concerning a strange, serpent-like creature inhabiting the waters of Bear Lake, which they say carried off some of their braves many moons ago. Since then, they will not sleep close to the lake. Neither will they swim in it, nor let their squaws and papooses bathe in it.

Now, it seems this water devil, as the Indians called it, has again made an appearance. A number of our white settlers declare they have seen it with their own eyes. This Bear Lake Monster, they now call it, is causing a great deal of excitement up here. S. M. Johnson at South Eden was riding along near the Lake the other day when he saw something a number of yards out in the lake which he thought was the body of a man. He waited for the waves to wash it in, but to his surprise, found the water washed over it without causing it to move. Then he saw it had a head and neck like some strange animal. On each side of the head were ears, or bunches the size of a pint cup. He concluded the body must be touching the bottom of the lake. By this time, however, Johnson seems to have been leaving the place so rapidly he failed to observe other details.

The next day three women and a man saw a monstrous animal in the lake near the same place, but this time it was swimming at an incredible speed. According to their statement, it was moving faster than a horse could run.

On Sunday last, N. C. Davis and Allen Davis of St. Charles; Thomas Sleight and James Collings of Paris, with six women were returning from Fish Haven when about midway from the latter place to St. Charles, their attention was suddenly attracted to a peculiar motion of waves on the water about three miles distant. The lake was not rough, only a little disturbed by the wind. Mr. Sleight says he distinctly saw the sides of a very large animal that he would suppose to be not less than 90 feet in length. Mr. Davis doesn't think he saw any part of the body, but is positive it must not have been less than forty feet in length, judging by the waves it rolled up on both sides of it as it swam, and the wave it left in the rear. It was going south, and all agreed it swam with a speed almost incredible to their senses. Mr. Davis says he never saw a locomotive travel faster, and thinks it made a mile a minute. In a few minutes after the discovery of the first, a second followed in its wake, but seemed much smaller, appearing to Mr. Sleight about the size of a horse. A larger one followed this, and so on until before disappearing, made a sudden turn to the west a short distance, then back to its former track. At this turn Mr. Sleight says he could distinctly see it was of a brown color. They could judge somewhat of the speed by observing known distances on the opposite side of the lake;

and all agree that the velocity with which these monsters propelled themselves, was astounding. They represent the waves rolling up on each side as about three feet high. This is substantially their statement as they told me. Messengers Davis and Sleight are prominent men, well known in the country, and all of them are reliable persons, whose veracity is undoubted. I have no doubt they would be willing to make affidavits to their statements.

The report electrified Salt Lake City, where a newspaper reporter soon was assigned to follow up and ask people around Bear Lake what they thought. That reporter said he "quizzed many Bear Lake people and found hardly a person who doubted it."

Bear Lake has been said to be home to an indigenous monster, though descriptions of it vary.

For a generation to come, the Bear Lake Monster was refer-enced publicly in both Idaho and Utah and seemed to be taken at least somewhat seriously. Both major newspapers in Salt Lake City, the *Deseret News* and the *Salt Lake Tribune*, delivered periodic references to it, sometimes noting alleged sightings, and on other occasions trying to debunk them.

The push for giving it credibility was, unusually enough, given some push by the LDS Church. In the October 10, 1868, entry for one official church report, "President Young's Trip North," an entry headed "The monsters of Bear Lake" reported this:

We have had conversation with Brother Charles C. Rich and other brethren from Bear Lake Valley, respecting the monsters which have been seen in the Lake, an account of which, from the pen of brother Joseph C. Rich, was published in the Evening News a short time ago. They all firmly believe the account as published. They consider the testimony that has been given by so many individuals, who have seen these creatures in so many places and under a variety of circumstances, indisputable. They would believe these persons upon any other subject, and they cannot withhold their credence—incredible as the existence of such monsters may appear—from what they say they saw in the Lake. We should conclude that there are very few, if any, persons in Bear Lake Valley who doubt the statements that have been made. The Indian traditions corroborate all that has been said of these creatures. It is well known that the Indians will not camp near the Lake, and they have never been known to bathe in its waters. They have persisted in stating that there were terrible monsters in the Lake, of which they were in fear, two of their tribe having, within the memory of some of their number, been carried off by them.

The discussion didn't stop at recounting stories. The settlers were also trying to develop an action plan for going after the monster, or monsters. From the official 1868 church report:

Various plans have been suggested for the capture of one or more of them, but no attempt has yet been made. We hope that some plan may be devised that will be successful. Until the question of their existence is settled, and something learned of their nature and habits, if such monsters are actually there, the Lake will not be a very common place of resort for fishermen. One of those who are said to have seen them last, timed their speed while passing from one well known point to another on the other side of the Lake, with his watch, and if the description can be relied upon, a boat would stand no chance of escaping if they were pursued or came into contact with it.

The report did conclude, tongue in cheek, that the reports were "fishy." But no firm decisions were made.

The story cooled off during the next couple of decades. In 1894, an older Joseph Rich confessed in a public talk that the discussion of the monster a generation earlier actually had been "a wonderful first class lie." That might seem to have ended the subject. And yet the monster refused to go away.

Those who submitted a letter to the editor of the newspaper in Logan, Utah, on September 10, 1907, said that when they camped lakeside, the Bear Lake Monster had attacked the camp and even killed one of their horses.

In 1937, another witness claimed to have seen the monster personally. He was just four years old at the time. But nine years later, a Boy Scout leader camping at the lake made a similar report.

In 2002, a businessman named Brian Hirschi, who worked near the lake, maintained that he saw it . . . or something like it. Hirschi was the operator of a pontoon boat, made up to look like a lake monster, which he used to carry tourists on trips around the lake. He was wrapping up a trip when he saw what looked like "two humps in the water," and then, "The next thing I know, a serpent-like creature shot up out of the water." He said it looked dark green and slimy, and it had red eyes. Then, he said, it vanished. Skeptics—and there were skeptics—pointed out that Hirschi did, after all, have a stake in the tourist trade. And the monster story.

An episode of Animal Planet's *Lost Tapes* TV series (season 2, episode 9, in November 2009) was devoted to the Bear Lake Monster, after which its national visibility spiked. It was also featured on the SyFy Channel program *Haunted Highway* (season 1, episode 1, in 2012) in an episode called "Bear Lake Beast; Vergas Hairy Man."

The latter program, in its segment on Bear Lake, featured an underwater journey, in which divers said they had located a large bone from a cow in an underwater cave and wondered how it got there. The question remained unresolved.

A July 2004 news story by the Associated Press took a more evenhanded view, saying:

> Its very existence has been debated at coffee shops and campfires since the first published report of its existence in 1868. The only thing is, people can't seem to agree on the details. Some say it looks like a walrus minus the tusks; others are adamant it's a dinosaur or a big alligator that swims really fast. The only thing not in question is the monster's ability to make cash registers sing at stores ringing the lake on the Idaho-Utah border.

That it does. Besides the Bear Lake Monster boat, the source of one of the sightings, there's a float in an annual Raspberry Days parade held in Garden City, Utah, immediately south of the Idaho-Utah line, and also fronting on Bear Lake. The parade features local children—referred to cheerfully as "the real Bear Lake monsters"—and a variety of events. One year the participating children were invited to name the monster. For reasons unclear, the choice was to call it "Isabella." That is apparently the only name the monster in this lake has ever gotten.

Tourism at Bear Lake, in fact, has been doing just fine.

CHAPTER 4

Updyke's Treasure

Somewhere, possibly in the more remote reaches of the eastern Magic Valley or in the Raft River country, there lies hidden—in all probability—a cache of gold and other precious materials from one of the most successful stagecoach robberies of the Old West.

It was one of the most successful and also one of the most unusual robberies because one of the culprits, possibly the gang's leader, was none other than the sheriff of the territory's largest county. But its success was short-lived: The robbers may never have gotten an opportunity to spend their ill-gotten gains.

Idaho was not the scene of many of the West's more spectacular robberies; many of the Rocky Mountain states have more of those tales to tell. But in territorial days plenty of money was stolen in Idaho, and there's no lack of treasure supposedly still out there, waiting to be found in obscure corners of the Gem State.

In south-central Idaho near the remote—it remains tough to reach even now—and tiny community of Three Creek, a rancher was said to have allowed his home to be used by robbers as a way station and rest point, in return for a skim off their takings. After one big robbery, which supposedly netted $40,000 in coins, the robbers fell out while at their hideaway; one was killed, and another fled the country. The coins remained hidden. The rancher and an orphan boy who lived with him worried about the possibility of retaliation or other follow-up violence, and kept quiet about what they knew. If they did know exactly where the stash was hidden, they didn't say, and apparently never spent it. Decades later, after the rancher was long dead, the orphan told the story to friends. The easily checkable details matched the facts—there was a large robbery of coins when and where he reported it, and the robbers weren't caught. But the coins were never found.

Remote and lightly populated—then and now—Clark County was the scene of a $50,000 robbery treasure deposit, or so the story goes. This one was attributed to George Ives, an active robber long tied to the Montana outlaw and lawman Henry Plummer. Ives, caught for at least some of his crimes, wound up in the Idaho Penitentiary. He told one of the guards that after he robbed a stagecoach in Clark County he was soon pursued by a posse. Realizing he might be caught—as he was—he buried the $50,000 in cash along his getaway route. He drew a crude map and gave it to the guard, in hopes it could be recovered. The guard journeyed to eastern Idaho, but a couple of key landmarks had changed, and he could never find the exact spot. The money, if it was ever there, may still be buried in the county's hot springs area.

Modest amounts of gold have been found in the world-famous Silver Valley, in the Idaho Panhandle, and it may have been there in 1888, about the time big silver finds were located. That year, prospector Zak Stoneman dug up a pile of the yellow stuff and headed west to sell it. Traveling near Priest Lake, his mules chowed down on poisonous weeds and died. Unable to transport the gold any farther, Stoneman buried it nearby. Later he returned to the area to collect it, but even after a series of long and frustrating searches, neither he nor a number of other people who followed after could find it.

There's another legend that the robber Butch Cassidy, separately from his possible hit of a bank in Montpelier (see chapter 13), hid some of his loot along a path in northern Idaho, somewhere between what is now eastern Spokane and Wallace, not far from what is now I-90. There were no more specific indicators, though, and no such money has ever been found. And it seems unlikely; this is a part of the country where Cassidy sightings were considered more rumor than fact.

All of these buried treasures have to take a back seat, however, to the most unusual. What may have been the largest haul and surely one of the most dramatic of the missing treasure stories may be that of the lost treasure of David C. Updyke. His story illuminates the difficulty not so much of obtaining the stolen money but of keeping it afterward.

Like Plummer—whose story was well known in the region— Updyke was both a lawman and an outlaw. Like Plummer, he was born and raised in the northeastern United States and was drawn to California by the gold rush. Like Plummer too, Updyke was soon distracted by new gold strikes and opportunities in the Northwest. Plummer was active in the Lewiston area in northern Idaho for a time; when he left for Montana, some of his men drifted south to the new boom area around Idaho City and Boise. There they met Updyke, who helped organize them into what was, for a time, an effective criminal organization.

That was Updyke's night job. His day work was that of a pillar of the community. He invested some of the money he had made in California in a new saloon in Boise, and when Ada County (of which Boise is the seat) was formed in 1865, his night and day worlds merged. Updyke was elected the first sheriff of the new county in March of that year. His role as a businessman in town gave him surface respectability, while his badge offered protection to the outlaws. But he also moonlighted as, among other things, a road robber.

Updyke participated in many robbery jobs over the years, but the biggest, and the one that indirectly led to his downfall, was instigated by a man named Brockie Jack. Jack was a well-known "road agent"—which is to say highway robber—whose exploits had been reported in newspapers up and down the Pacific coast. California became too hot to hold him, and his robberies in Oregon finally resulted in arrest and incarceration there. Escaping from jail there, he decided to head inland and try a community where local law enforcement was friendlier to professionals of his kind: Boise.

One day in May 1865, he rode into downtown Boise and walked, no doubt as inconspicuously as possible, into Updyke's saloon. There he sat down with Sheriff Updyke and two associated gunmen, Willy Wittmore and Fred Williams, all men of varied temperaments and perspectives. Updyke was a cool schemer; Wittmore was well-known for his quick, hot temper but also his willingness to act; Williams was an eager would-be professional.

With them, he hoped to strike a deal. And he did.

We don't know how that conversation evolved—no one, obviously, took minutes—but the discussion turned to a stage line that was still in its first few months of operation. It ran from the goldfields of Montana south to the urban service centers of Salt Lake City, the nearest location where gold could be converted into spending cash. The route passed through eastern Idaho not far from present-day I-15. The attraction, obviously, was the gold and cash the stages carried, and the line's weaknesses in the area of security. The stage line moved irregularly, though, and any attempt to get at the contents would mean the road agents would have to be patient.

The conspirators—Jack, Wittmore, Williams, and Updyke—took off for eastern Idaho at the end of May. They waited for weeks in the desert sun, camping near the old and even-then dilapidated Fort Hall, by the banks of Ross Fork Creek. Over those weeks they checked with contacts in Montana to find out when the stage was leaving. When it did, in late July, the robbers were ready.

They had researched the details of how the shipments worked, and they knew what people were traveling: an easygoing driver named Charlie Parks, a young Mormon couple headed back home to Utah, and a gambler. They also had an accomplice of their own inside the coach as it headed south.

On July 26, on its fifth day south, well inside Idaho and loaded with both gold and passengers, the stage gingerly made the crossing of Ross Fork Creek (not far from present-day Fort Hall) and then stopped. A couple of large boulders had been rolled into the path, and they would have to be removed. It was an immediate warning of danger, but there was no choice: They'd have to stop and move them.

When they did, Jack, Williams, and Wittmore stepped into plain sight, their firearms at the ready. Updyke apparently remained, at first, out of view, held in reserve.

Stagecoach robberies were not rare in southern Idaho in early territorial days. This stagecoach picture was taken near the Idaho border at what is now Yellowstone National Park.
THE LIBRARY OF CONGRESS

What might have been a relatively simple robbery almost immediately became more complex. One of the passengers was a professional gambler named Sam Martin, and when he saw from inside the coach what was happening, he leaned out the window and called out—something. His few words are lost, but we know he quickly followed them with a small handgun, which he aimed and fired at Wittmore.

The bullet hit Wittmore in the hand, enough to hurt him but not enough to stop him. Quickly infuriated, he lifted own weapon and fired back at the coach, not one or twice but over and over, reloading over a couple of minutes. He did not stop to consider that his own accomplice inside the coach was one of the targets. Finally, Brockie Jack reached him and pulled the gun away from him.

It was too late. The initial exchange had started a mass shoot-out and extensive killing. The driver and one of the passengers were able to flee into the hills. Five passengers—the couple from Utah among them—lay dead, and one more appeared to be dead but wasn't; he hoped to escape their attention. The onboard accomplice was dead, and Williams was shot in the arm.

Jack surveyed the scene and called out, "My God, they're all dead!"

They may have paused in shock for a bit, but probably not long. Their careful scoping of the shipment had suggested a rich take could be had, and it was. They found fifteen big bars of gold, all carefully marked and numbered, and bags of gold dust; the value was estimated at $86,000. In 1865 terms, it was an enormous haul, the robbery of a lifetime, one of the biggest of the period.

The robbers packed their take and rode back toward Boise. Somewhere along the way they deposited—probably buried—their loot. They had failed, however, to clean up after themselves at the robbery site. They had left witnesses behind.

From a viewpoint in the hills above the stage road, driver Charlie Parks and the one uninjured passenger watched the proceedings as they kept out of view. When the robbers departed, they made their way back to the stage, where the not-yet-dead passenger was given some aid and eventually recovered. The three of them slowly moved along the stage route toward Boise and stopped at a station along the way.

As they traveled, they compared notes. And they found they knew who their robbers were. Parks, who had extensive experience driving stagecoaches around the region, recognized both Brockie Jack and David Updyke. The left-for-dead passenger had recognized the other two, Williams and Wittmore.

Moving carefully, working through connections, they made contact with the company insuring the shipment. With names attached to the deed, the insurer offered a $10,000 reward contingent on finding the gold and arresting the robbers.

One never happened, and the other took time.

Updyke was still sheriff of Ada County, and that presented a problem for anyone trying to arrest him. He was, however, already under pressure. A local group of vigilantes based on the Payette River northwest of Boise already had formed to try to oust him. Only a few months into Updyke's term of office, pressure was on the Ada County commission to do something about him.

Their first effort along those lines was a new election, ordered by the commission and held shortly after the eastern Idaho stage robbery in August, just after Updyke had spent much of his time out of town. The election brought several new officials into play, including the county's first district attorney, a lawyer named Albert Heed. The voters also chose a new sheriff, rejecting Updyke in favor of John Duvall, who was part-owner of a Boise River ferry. There was a catch: Legally the new terms could not begin until the new year, and until then, Updyke still would have a free hand.

The commissioners had another tactic in mind, though. At that time, the sheriff was also the chief tax collector in the county, and Updyke—as might be expected—had sticky fingers when it came to turning over to the treasury everything he had collected. (This may have been the first action that turned the county powers against him, faster than the road robberies.) In September, just a few weeks after the election, the commission insisted that Heed file charges against Updyke. Fearful of the gunslingers who might not react well to that, Heed instead resigned his new job and left town.

The commissioners, unfazed, appointed a new prosecutor and gave him the same instructions. They also ordered Duvall—who was not yet legally a sheriff but still a private citizen—to arrest Updyke.

Legally that made no sense, but Duvall turned out to be as remarkable and fearless a character as Heed had failed to be. With nothing more than the goodwill of the county commission, he rounded up a posse—probably members of the Payette vigilante group were among them—and confronted Updyke, then escorted him into his own jail and locked him in a cell. The new prosecutor then called a grand jury to decide what to charge Updyke with.

Days later, Updyke appeared in court, pointed out that he was unlawfully restrained and was still the lawfully elected sheriff, and persuaded the judge to release him after posting a bond, which he did. Updyke walked back into his sheriff's office to resume business.

The case against him still didn't go away, however, and on October 5 he was scheduled to go back to court to appear before a judge on the tax theft and other issues.

He had been a cool malefactor up to this point, but now it seemed the stress had gotten to him. Apparently he decided to try to get out from under the web of charges he faced, so he made a deal with the county: He would return the errant tax money to the county and resign as sheriff, in return for the county leaving him alone. He carried through on the first two parts, and the commission appears to have followed through on the second by appointing as the new sheriff not Duvall, who would have gone after Updyke, but rather one of Updyke's deputies, William West. That essentially gave Updyke freedom of movement for the next couple of months, until Duvall took office.

Updyke might have fled, collected his share of the treasure, and found another remote part of the West in which to hide out, but he instead stayed in Boise. Just after the turn of the year, word came to town about military conflict with one of the Indian tribes in the area. Updyke was still popular enough that he could and did raise a regiment of volunteers—presumably including much of the old gang—purchased horses to ride, and headed off to battle. It seems to have been an excuse, because the group did not see any conflict. Updyke, however, had a theoretically legitimate band of protectors in Boise, and Duvall and others who wanted him arrested were again stymied.

But only briefly, because this was a group without a lot of self-discipline. One of the sellers of horses to Updyke's unit filed a civil suit in court, saying he hadn't been paid for them. A trial was held, and during it one of Updyke's troopers, Reuben Reynolds, let slip that the military unit was really just another cover (much as the sheriff's office had been) for gang activities. Shortly after that, another of Updyke's men, John Clark, shot Reynolds to death. That finally gave Duvall a clear line of action: He quickly arrested and imprisoned Clark.

This put Updyke in a bind, because he had to be seen as supporting his men. He started to issue threats about what he might do if Clark wasn't released. That was a mistake, since Clark's guilt was so well established. Popular support for Updyke almost vanished, and most of his support crowd melted away.

Within days, on April 12, Updyke and one of his few remaining friends, Jake Dixon, quietly slipped out of Boise, heading into the mountains in the northeast.

The Danskin Mountains were, at the time, just beginning to be explored for precious metals mining. Gold was found in the streams there in late 1863, and a small gold rush ensued in the next couple of years. The remote mountain mining settlements of Atlanta and Rocky Bar were becoming busy enough, with enough wealth passing through to attract the likes of Updyke.

His movements were being watched, however, and a party from Boise had taken off after him to track him down. They had little difficulty finding him through either the winter snow or the talkative residents.

In mid-April, Updyke and Dixon reached an abandoned cabin near Syrup Creek, high in the mountains. They had rested there perhaps a night or two when they were surrounded and captured by the posse from Ada County. When the posse left, Updyke and Dixon were hanging from nooses in a shed nearby. Updyke is said to have had just $50 in his pockets when he was hanged.

So, within a year of one of the most profitable stage robberies of the era, the gang leader was dead. The three other participants all disappeared from view: Jack, Williams, and Wittmore had scattered and were not heard from nor ever seen again in Idaho; and in the short remaining period while they were still visible, they never showed any signs of particular wealth. Updyke, as canny as he was, likely would have taken some precaution to ensure that no one of them could have run off with it.

There was never an indication that any of them collected any wealth. What happened to it? There's been some talk that the robbers, looking for an obscure and little-traveled place to stash their loot, might have headed for the City of Rocks, south of Albion. But that's just a guess.

Somewhere out there, it is very likely that a highly valuable stash of gold is still just waiting for someone to come to collect it.

CHAPTER 5

Spirit Lake

The war declared by the Kootenai Tribe of Idaho on September 20, 1974, against the United States of America, came much later than the reputed haunting of Spirit Lake, but it sheds some light on why people still pay attention to the body of water, and also pay close attention to some of the buildings overlooking it.

The war was declared by the sixty-seven members of the tribe; it apparently was, in other words, unanimous.

The road to war started with the election of Amy Trice to the tribal council and after that to the chairmanship. Working with a tribal administrator, she sought federal help with housing, roads and other repair and upgrade items, and other assistance to compensate for the steady whittling away of their tribal lands, now reduced to a small area near the city of Bonners Ferry. Conditions on the reservation were poor; illness of various kinds was raging. She was told the tribe was too small to qualify for most types of assistance.

In an interview years later, she said, "That made me mad. Doug [Wheaton, tribal official] and I discussed it and decided there was no place else to go. So we said, 'let's go to war.' We said it jokingly but it turned serious and we did go to war."

No shots were fired. The tribe set up roadblocks at which their guards would ask for payment to enter the reservation. The story about this, even in the pre-Internet days, went international, and the tribe began winning some federal benefits. After a few more years, the tribe would open a prosperous hotel, and later a casino was attached to it. In more recent years, the tribe has prospered.

Those developments were not especially unusual among Indian tribes in the late twentieth century, or even among the tribes in Idaho. The Kootenai Tribe was, however, unusual in other respects than simply declaring (and winning) a public relations war.

Their tribal shield, a kind of logo, includes an image of a sheet of paper with space for, but containing no, signatures. That reflects the piece of tribal history that includes—rare among Native Americans—no treaty settlement with the United States. The Kootenai of Idaho (there is a Montana group as well) live on a reservation, but unusual among regional tribes, the reservation was built around their home location; they were not moved away from their traditional lands. The links of location are particularly strong here.

They had their reasons for insisting on staying put, one of them relating to their religious beliefs. No treaty, they felt, should ever contravene the sacred covenant that was a part of their origin story. As the tribe's website explains it, "Kootenai elders pass down the history of the beginning of time, which tells that the Kootenai people were created by Quilxka Nupika, the Supreme Being, and placed on earth to keep the Creator-Spirit's Covenant—to guard and keep the land forever."

The creation story of the seven bands of the Kootenai is complex. The people called the Kootenai—there have been other spellings, including Kootenay or Kutenai—derive the name from the description of the group as the "Water People." That might seem an odd description for people located so far from the ocean or large bodies of water, but it related directly to waters that did run in the Idaho Panhandle. The strongest connection was with the Kootenai River, which flows through Bonners Ferry and through the reservation lands.

It also, however, connects them to another body of water, some miles to the southwest, called Spirit Lake. It is not one of the largest lakes in the area; at just under twenty-four hundred acres, Spirit Lake is far smaller than the better-known Coeur d'Alene and Pend Oreille Lakes. Nor is it unusually deep: only about one hundred feet in many places.

But it does have some unusual characteristics. Spirit Lake is located in a "snow belt," a microclimate area that receives more snow than most of the surrounding territory. That deposit—when the snow from the mountains that surround the lake turns each spring into runoff—may have been part of the reason the Kootenai also called it "Clear Water."

The lake has another unusual quality: It is fully enclosed, something like a man-made swimming pool. Its floor is sealed in clay, somewhat similar to sealants of some private ponds, except that this one—a rare example of the type—is natural. The city of Spirit Lake proclaims, "Spirit Lake is reputed to be one of only two lakes in the world with a sealed bottom—an apt location for those phantom spirits that are said to haunt the beautiful waters of this fascinating Lake of the Spirits."

The lake is notably alive with plants and animals and has a remarkably wide array of fish, from kokanee salmon to perch, catfish, sunfish, and various types of trout.

The sealed bottom may, however, change the chemistry of Spirit Lake compared to many other lakes, which might help account for some of the unusual phenomena sometimes seen there.

There are of course other explanations.

The Kootenai once called it "Clear Water," fitting for its role as a high mountain lake. But it came to be associated with another old name, Tesemini, which may be a word that originated from far away, among the Salish people. Tesemini was thought to be an early spirit of the lake. (Or, by some other etymological accounts, *tesemini* simply means "lake of the spirits.")

The Kootenai creation story says that the people of the tribe were formed by Quilxka Nupika, regarded as the Supreme Being. The story said the people were put in place to maintain and take care of the earth, and to stay in their place as guardians. The obligation was meant to last permanently. That is one reason the Kootenai never signed a treaty, never agreed to be relocated to another reservation site, and still live generally where they traditionally did. The main difference is that the Kootenai formerly roamed over a much larger area, which included the region around Spirit Lake.

The story of the tribe's early days tells of the difficulty in those times staying in place and maintaining the land. One of those talks of a man called "Good Chieftain"—Hyas-Tyee-Skookum-Tum-Tum—who lived not far from Spirit Lake. Good Chieftain had a daughter, Hya-Pam, or "Fearless Running Water"; her beauty was widely remarked, and would lead to tragedy. She fell in love with a Kootenai brave named Hasht-Eel-Ame-Hoom, or "Shining Eagle." They planned to make a life together, but regional politics intervened.

East of the Kootenai territory, another tribe, a hostile tribe, had settled and begun to impinge on the Kootenai territory. The tribe was powerful enough to threaten the Kootenai's existence, but the elderly chief, named Pu-Pu-Mox-Mox (or "Yellow Serpent"), offered a deal. If the daughter of the Kootenai chief were given to him in marriage, he pledged, he would leave the Kootenai alone.

Good Chieftain reluctantly agreed to the terms. Fearless Running Water did not. She and Shining Eagle determined that they could not and would not be separated. They broke off from the tribe and eloped to the lake. There, they are said to have bound themselves in what was called a "marriage chain of rushes." Pledging eternal devotion, the couple climbed Suicide Cliff (evidently named for this story), which overlooked the lake, jumped off, and dove in. They were never seen again. (What became of Good Chieftain's tribe in the wake of his failure to come through on the deal with Yellow Serpent remains something of a mystery.)

One story has it that the spirit Tesemini was already there, living deep within the lake, and offered to help them; and from that point they wandered the lake, sometimes flying above it up in the air, reminding the people of the area of their story, mystifying people who visit Spirit Lake to this day. Or so it is said.

Or maybe the spirit Tesemini was originally aroused by them, and they merged with it and created a new spiritual climate in the lake.

Or one of the other variations. In any of those, the lake is said to be—in some sense at least—haunted. As a Spirit Lake website put it, "Folklore tells us that on a moonlit night, when the wind is still, you may see their shadowy silhouettes as they drift across the lake in a phantom canoe. As the lake ice floes melt and grind together in springtime, weird, mournful, and haunting sounds are heard, are these the cries of the Indian lovers as they seek release from the Lake of the Spirits?"

Another version of this story was reported by a local radio station on its website:

People often report of seeing the two on nights where the moon lights up the lake. Many sightings of the young lovers' ghostly silhouettes drifting across the lake in a canoe have been reported. When investigated . . . no canoe is found and no bodies.

In the Spring a foggy mist hovers above the lake and through the mist you'll hear a low, spooky moaning sound. It's distinct and clear but seeing through the mist and fog is impossible. Legend says the moans are the two lovers crying out to seek freedom from the Spirit of the Lakes, but that freedom never comes.

Stephen Lindsay, writing in the August 23, 2007, Spokane *Spokesman-Review*, said, "Spirit Lake, possibly because Tesemini isn't happy with development, has not had as progressive a history as most parts of Kootenai County. There are roughly 12 miles of shoreline to the lake itself, but most of this is privately owned and not accessible by road." Most development is on the northeast side of the lake.

There is another tale of haunting at Spirit Lake, not of the body of water but in the town, in that development on one part of the

The town center of Spirit Lake, with the White Horse Saloon and Hotel on the right.
Jon Roanhaus

lakeshore. The town itself is sometimes said to be overseen by old spirits, and a certain calming spirit does feel as if it's in the air.

Spirit Lake is a small city, located on the northeast shore of the same-named body of water. It is located miles away from the Kootenai reservation (and of the city's 1,300 or so residents, only nine—as of the 2000 census—were Native American, and not all of them Kootenai).

The Kootenai were long gone from the area, which is in the northern reach of the Rathdrum Prairie, by the time dryland farmers from points west and south showed up in the 1880s. It was an agricultural region until, around the turn of the century, the Panhandle Lumber Company, under the ownership of Frank

Blackwell, appeared and launched a large timber operation. Among other entities, he formed the Spirit Lake Land Company, and bought about twenty-five thousand acres in the Spirit Lake area.

Blackwell built a large sawmill starting in 1907, designed to handle a variety of wood projects. His associated land company laid out a plat for the town of Spirit Lake, a place where workers and others associated with them could live and commerce could be conducted—within limits of course, since Spirit Lake was then very much a company town. By 1910 the town was reported to have as many as one thousand residents and more than one hundred buildings. (Commuting from much farther away wasn't practical in those days.) Over the next decade or so, the town's population more than doubled.

Blackwell seems to have had higher ambitions for Spirit Lake, because his next step was to build a railroad—at least a part of the Idaho and Washington Northern Railroad, which ran south to the city of Rathdrum and from there to Newport, Washington, and beyond. It turned out to be good investment for Blackwell, because only a few years later, in 1916, the rail line was bought by Chicago, Milwaukee and St. Paul Railroad for $5 million, much more than Blackwell had spent on building it.

The book *Historical Spirit Lake, Idaho and Vicinity* (by Keith and Jan Spencer) reflects a community that got started with a big boost and then rolled along quietly. For a generation, the Spirit Lake timber operations continued profitably; at the time Blackwell died in 1922, his business appeared to remain in stable condition. Wood was taken from around the region—not much near the lake itself—and shipped out by rail.

In 1939, a massive forest fire roared down from the east near one of the major timber locations, Mount Spokane, and reached the edges of the town of Spirit Lake. A heroic effort in town was able to stop it just shy of the main part of town. But though the timber mill operation was saved, the railroad was not, and its operations were turned to ash. The loss was too large even to contemplate a rebuild, and eventually the timber operation too shut down. What once was the office building for the Panhandle Lumber Company, located near the mill's old pond, eventually was turned into the Fireside Lodge.

After the 1940s, the town of Spirit Lake became much quieter. It reverted in part to its agricultural roots, but after the twentieth century reached its midpoint, Spirit Lake—the water body—became a popular vacation and second-home spot for residents in the growing Spokane and Coeur d'Alene areas.

The city has noted on its website:

> The shores of Spirit Lake served as a site for summer homes for several years. Later, the summer people became year-round residents. City residents are now listed at approximately 900 in 1989, but lake residents boost the population to nearly triple that number. New construction is progressing. In the mid 70s a move was made to create an Old West appearance to the businesses on Maine Street. The city still serves as a bedroom community for workers employed elsewhere and still retains its small-town atmosphere.

The city of Spirit Lake has a quiet lakeside park, used primarily for local soccer and volleyball games. But by the lakeshore a historical sign notes the old story of the spirit haunting the lake.

The lake and nearby town are in a pretty setting, and visitors do come by. An article in the Spokane *Spokesman-Review* noted, "Today the lake is known mainly for its fishing, and the Silver Beach Resort is still in operation. The area has also become known among mountain bikers and hikers as the back door into the eastern wilds of Mount Spokane via the Brickle Creek Valley. The mountain itself dominates the view to the west from the lake."

The old stories about the haunted lake gave the community some extra cachet. But that was not the only specific haunting story around town; maybe the town's name encourages their telling.

Some of it is just the atmosphere. *Spokesman-Review* correspondent Lindsay said, "I live across the alley from an old, haunted theater. There are nights when my kids have trouble getting to sleep because of this. So, to me it's a wonder that anyone can sleep, or even dares go out at night, around Spirit Lake."

The best-known local haunted story concerns the town's oldest lodgings. The White Horse Hotel, Saloon & Cafe, located on Maine Street (named after the state, as opposed to indicating a prime thoroughfare), is prominent in the center of downtown Spirit Lake, about three blocks from the waterfront. It has been described as the oldest continuously operating hotel in Idaho (others started earlier, but have had extended periods of closure). It was launched in 1907—alongside the construction of the Panhandle sawmill—and remains highly active today. It has operated under other names in the past, but it has been the White Horse for more than thirty years. Rooms are available for rent, and there's a busy saloon downstairs.

And for about a century, the place has earned its place as a true resident of Spirit Lake. It was sometime in the 1920s when stories of the haunting there are said to have begun. One description in a site about Idaho hauntings said that "the spirit is known affectionately to staff and locals as 'Big Girl' and she is responsible for slamming doors and moving items throughout the hotel. She has also appeared as an apparition on a number of occasions. She seems to be especially drawn to Room 2 of the hotel."

Dolli Massener, who has lived almost all her life in Spirit Lake and has worked at the White Horse for many years, said that she personally has occasionally had "an acquaintance with the Big Girl, as I call her." She said the spirit turns up in barely visible form, "as a shadow or something," but the Big Girl has been physically active too. "She's thrown plates at me and done strange things," she said. "She likes to pull jokes on people."

The story behind her, Massener said, is a tale that sounds about a century old. It maintains that she was once employed in the hotel and spent many hours there cleaning the guest rooms. One day—and presumably when she was in Room 2—her young son was with her, but then ran off, downstairs, and outside the hotel. "He got away from her and ran into the street, and he was run over by a horse and buggy, and was killed." What happened after that to the young mother is unclear. But the story would explain the emotional link to the old hotel.

The Spirit Lake stories are not among the best known of those around Idaho—the community never has become one of Idaho's top tourist draws, despite the pretty location—but they have persisted for many years and word of them has spread.

In 2015, a novelist named Brooklyn Ann released a story called "Tesemini: Lake of Spirits." The book's story was described in the website Goodreads this way:

Aspiring heavy metal band, Rage of Angels, have found a perfect place to practice their music: an abandoned church in Spirit Lake, Idaho. But once they set up their gear on the vacant altar, a barrage of eerie occurrences threaten to drive the band out of their new sanctuary. When they discover that the church is haunted by enraged ghosts of the Kootenai Indian tribe, they utilize the advice of a voodoo priestess to confront the angry spirits.

But that's another story.

CHAPTER 6

The President of Pardee

The house, visible from far away across the river, did not have the look of a classic mansion exactly, because it was a little too low-slung and relaxed. But it fit its landscape, and it looked elegant, almost serene. Situated on a gently sloping, tree-lined hillside, it had a large "rustic front porch" wrapped partway around the building. The porch and the windows behind it looked south and below across the gently flowing Clearwater River and the narrow valley it anchored. It was commonly regarded as the finest-looking house in the Clearwater Valley, and, over the years, many people in the area visited to see it up close, and they often remarked on how finely it was furnished.

That house stuck in memory, and people who grew up in the area never forgot it. It was clear in the memory of the writer of a 2015 letter to the nearby *Lewiston Morning Tribune*. He had grown up in Orofino, a dozen miles or so to the west and downstream along the Clearwater River; his mother had been born in Orofino in 1911 and lived there all the years since. He recalled her saying, "The illegitimate daughter of one of our presidents lived in it when she was a child."

That description was at least slightly off—the gender was wrong even in the broadly spread rumors—and it may have been altogether wrong, but the essence of it has been accepted in outline by generations of residents in the area.

The house itself is gone now, demolished decades ago, as are all remnants of what once was the rail stop next to it, and in effect the small community of Pardee. Today, driving on Highway 12 between Kamiah and Kooskia, looking across the Clearwater River, you can see a slightly flattened area around a bend. This area once contained a small collection of houses and commercial buildings, as well as one of Idaho's enduring mysteries. Was this really the house bought by President Grover Cleveland for his mistress? So it was said, for many years, up and down the Clearwater Valley.

No sign, no marker, still exists to point out Pardee; and even if you did have a marker, you still could not easily get there even with four-wheel drive. There are no paved or even improved roads nearby on the north side of the river in that area. You'll need one of the better-detailed maps of the area even to find it. In its earlier years, a century ago, it was more easily reached.

The Clearwater River Valley was one of the earlier places in Idaho to experience settlement from eastern states. The triggering event in Idaho's formation as a territory, and its first big commercial rush—the gold rush at Pierce in 1862—occurred in the mountains on the north side of the Clearwater River; the river itself was usually gentle enough to allow for easy passage along the way. Permanent settlements along the riverside were slowed by issues surrounding the location and boundaries of the Nez Perce Indian reservation, but in 1895 much of the area was opened to settlement. A ferry service and a small town at what was called Orofino (derived from the mining activities but located downhill from them) appeared three years later.

There was plenty of commerce to bolster settlement. While the gold mining slowed down rapidly after the early strikes, the Clearwater River Valley, from Lewiston in the west (where the Clearwater merges with the Snake River) to Kooskia in the east, became a major timber production region by around 1900.

As soon as that demand for transportation services became clear, the would-be suppliers lined up to enter the field. A battle ensued among railroads over who should service the area, but ultimately the Northern Pacific Railway and Union Pacific Railroad joined forces to build several routes in the region, including one that ran from Lewiston up the Clearwater River as far as Stites, which was about as far as the river was navigable. A sprinkling of rail stops were designated, and one of these, between Orofino and Kamiah, was Pardee. Most of those stops, including Chapin and Tramway on either side of Pardee, disappeared decades ago as rail service diminished. The rail line ran on the north side of the Clearwater, opposite the current Highway 12, and road access on that north side today is rugged to nonexistent.

Pardee developed as a small rail stop, a place where local agricultural crops could be quickly loaded, and for a time passenger service developed too. It never grew into a substantial community, but a collection of residential and business buildings did emerge there early in the twentieth century.

It was most notable for that large, elegant house, so different from others in the area, the one with the spectacular porch and the sweeping river vista, and the collection of outbuildings near it, sitting atop a bluff overlooking the river. The landscaping was lush, with a deep lawn and fine rosebushes. It stood out distinctly from the usual run of logger and management homes, and for decades it just seemed to invite speculation.

The main house was more than three thousand square feet in size, much larger than most houses of the period, surrounded by a sweeping and covered deck. A living room anchored the main floor, and an elegant curved stairway connected it to two stories extended above, capped by a cupola providing skylight.

A 1990 retrospective in the *Lewiston Morning Tribune* noted that "Sister M. Alfreda Elsensohn, author of 'Pioneer Days in Idaho County,' visited the 'Bethmann Lodge' in 1937 and described it as 'a treasure house.' It was full of fine furniture, crystal, china, silver, brass, a grand piano, a library of books and display cases full of mementoes from all over the world." But the residents were something of a mystery.

So what had all that to do with Grover Cleveland? A good question, since Cleveland had no apparent personal Idaho connection.

Cleveland was born in New Jersey, in 1837, the son of a minister. The family moved while he was young, and he spent his formative years in Fayetteville, New York. His childhood years were hardscrabble, and when he moved to Buffalo, looking for any kind of work, he found a clerkship at a law firm. His natural determination took over, and he studied the law and after a few years became an attorney. Cleveland became a district attorney and sheriff, growing a reputation for hard work and personal honesty, and opposition to political machines such as Tammany Hall. The time would come when he would need to hang on to this reputation; it supplied much of his upward push in the absence of having many

This is one of the many political cartoons poking at the presidential candidate and then president Grover Cleveland over allegations that he fathered an illegitimate child.

of the important family, social, or business ties that many successful politicians did.

Rising quickly, he was elected mayor of Buffalo in 1881 and governor of New York only a year later; and in 1884, a deeply split Democratic Party nominated him for president. Cleveland's campaign slogan was "A public office is a public trust." And Cleveland's record in office generally supported that slogan. Opposition

Republicans soon had a few things to say about him personally, and developed a counter-slogan of their own.

Shortly before his election as Buffalo mayor, Cleveland had an affair with a widow named Maria Crofts Halpin. The circumstances surrounding the end of their relationship were, to say the least, disputed. She accused Cleveland of raping her. He denied that, and said that she was alcoholic and promiscuous. (Some things in politics really never do change.) Soon after, she had a child, and Cleveland, already influential in the area, pounced. He had Halpin sent to an institution, and the child was swooped up and sent to live with friends of his.

It was not an especially well-known story at first, known mainly in whispers around Buffalo. But that changed when Cleveland ran for president.

Helped by a minister in Buffalo who was familiar with the background of the Halpin case, Republican organizers in 1884 spread word about the illegitimate Halpin child and started a chant at their rallies: "Ma, Ma, where's my pa?" It was rapidly turned into a nationwide refrain. But it did not derail the Democratic candidacy. Showing an awareness of skilled public relations years ahead of his time, Cleveland countered by owning up to his paternity, or at least noting that he had been financially supporting the child and had been making payments to the mother. The widespread view seemed to be that he had made mistakes, but had in general made up for them.

When he won that 1884 election, marking the first Democratic win for the presidency in twenty-eight years, Democrats gleefully offered their own counter-chant: "Gone to the White House, ha, ha, ha!" All of that would have unlikely repercussions a couple of thousand miles away, in the northern part of Idaho, which wasn't even yet a state.

Cleveland was a bachelor when he arrived at the White House, but in 1885 he married Frances Folsom, whose family included old friends of Cleveland's. That marriage to an established society figure appeared to position Cleveland's personal life out of the realm of controversy.

The Folsoms were well-connected socially, and their friends included the wealthy Bethmann family in Boston. And that was a sign of just how well-connected they were, because the Bethmanns in turn were among the best-connected families not only in the United States but across Europe as well.

The Bethmann name dates to early medieval times, and was said to refer to someone who came from the Rhineland of Germany (although some records suggest the family tree may actually trace to the Netherlands). A Jurgen Bethke—the spelling of the name varied over time—was noted in the town registry of Oldenburg as far back as 1430. The family has a coat of arms dating to 1530, and family members gained prominence over the centuries that followed. They became noted continent-wide for their financial and mercantile enterprises. The Bethmann Bank AG in Frankfurt, founded in 1748 by Johann Philipp Bethmann and one of the earliest important banks in Germany, was described as "financier to the Prussian state"—it underwrote much of Germany's nine-teenth-century industrial revolution and helped finance the Eiffel Tower in Paris—and still operates today. It was considered for many years a close rival to the better-known House of Rothschild.

Bethmanns also held high governmental positions in Germany through the nineteenth century and into the World War I era.

The Bethmann family grew large, however, and some of its members decided to look for new opportunities overseas. One family member, Johann Ludwig Bethmann, came ashore in Philadelphia in 1774. The Cleveland connection, however, probably grew out of the arrival in New York, in 1864, of Marcus Bethmann, who had taken a ship from Bremen. The new branch of Bethmanns, presumably well staked, entered the import-export world of business in the United States; sugar seems to have been their major commercial interest.

Other members of the Bethmann family arrived from Germany (where they were said to be related to leading figures in the nobility) in 1880, and with money from their sugar manufacturing business there they started and built a new sugar import business in the United States. They would have become prominent in New York business and political circles about the same time Cleveland was, and would have moved in the same circles as his new wife.

Cleveland may be best known today for an electoral peculiarity more than for anything he did in office. To date, he is the only president to win two nonconsecutive terms: He won in 1884 and 1892, in between losing in 1888 to Republican Benjamin Harrison (who, as it would happen, was the president who signed the bill admitting Idaho into the union as a state). Then he defeated Harrison in an 1892 rematch.

During Cleveland's second term in office, one of the younger women in the Bethmann family, Frieda Bethmann (the daughter of Francis Alfred Ferdinand Bethmann and Emilie Bethmann), moved into the White House. Frieda Bethmann had been a close friend of Frances Folsom for years, and stayed until the Clevelands left the White House in early 1897. By some accounts she was a governess for the president's children; her mother had been active in promoting the then-new idea of kindergartens, and she was thought to have been in effect a kindergarten instructor at the White House. She was also described as an appointment secretary, though that seems more doubtful, and there are apparently no formal records to confirm her role there.

In 1898, the year after Cleveland's second term ended, Harry Bethmann, Frieda's brother and a mining engineer by profession, moved out west from his home in Boston.

He scouted around the mining districts in California and the Silver Valley in the Idaho Panhandle, and then decided the Clearwater River country held some promise. He did some work for the Northern Pacific Railroad, working on engineering and planning, and picked up a homestead tract next to the rail line, at Pardee.

Bethmann seems to have found the area fascinating. Geologically—which is how he would have looked at it—it was a seemingly mountainous area that was actually flatter than it looked, an area laced with deposits of basalt and diorite, a rock base much older in geologic time than most of Idaho. This part of the Clearwater Valley was along the western edge of the oldest version of what is now North America, many of tens of millions of years old.

He called his homestead the Red Gates Ranch but at first seemed to focus on prospects for mining silver, gold, or copper. He called that company Tri-Metallic Mines. The mining never amounted to much, but the house he had built there became something special. Once it was sufficiently completed for occupancy, Bethmann moved much of the rest of his family into it. The family included his mother Emilie, who some accounts say oversaw much of the work on the house. The newcomers also included his sister Frieda, not long departed from the Cleveland residence, along with her young son, Miner. (Or maybe he wasn't her son; at least one news report referred to him instead as her nephew.) Frieda Bethmann never married. Miner's paternity was not clearly established, and that would become a point of much discussion over the next century.

Specifically, the question went: Did Grover Cleveland have not one but two illegitimate children?

President Grover Cleveland may have had an Idaho connection running through a house in the community of Pardee, which once existed along this stretch of the Clearwater River in north-central Idaho.
RANDY STAPILUS

The Bethmanns were based in Pardee for many years, but family members traveled widely around the country and internationally. While the West had no lack of phony wealthy aristocrats prowling its backcountry, the Bethmanns were the real thing, and part of the evidence was that they didn't suck up the area's wealth; they added to it and invested in it. They were visible and active in Lewiston as well, where a 1951 obituary of Frieda Bethmann reported that "Miss Bethmann, until poor health prevented, was hostess at informal social affairs at the hotel."

Her son Miner attended a distant boarding school but returned to the Clearwater Valley as an adult and lived there until his death in 1982. He was active and prominent in the community, owning several businesses in Kooskia and Kamiah and working for the Potlatch Corporation.

The property in Pardee was largely gone before Miner's death. At some point after Frieda Bethmann's death, it was abandoned, and for a time its fine furnishings were picked at by thieves and vandals. The house was demolished in the 1960s, and its furnishings sold the decade after.

The legend around Pardee had to do with who Miner's father was. Was it Grover Cleveland? A number of items sold at auction had clear links to Cleveland. One was a silver box with the notation, "To Miner, from Grover Cleveland, 1904." There was also a 1906 note written by Frieda included in the Cleveland personal papers housed in the Library of Congress, which said simply, "My mother, Miner and I send our love and dearest good wishes, and may the coming year bring you health and happiness." (Cleveland's health didn't last long, unfortunately; he died in June 1908.)

Then there's the hotel register.

The register for the (now long-gone) Buster House hotel in Pomeroy, Washington, located west of the Clearwater Valley but also on a rail line, includes on Sunday, March 31, 1895, the name of Grover Cleveland, residence in Washington, D.C., as having paid for a room. This was of course several years before the Bethmanns came to Pardee, but was Cleveland there for a related purpose?

The signature actually didn't look a lot like Cleveland's, and the name wasn't an especially rare one at the time in any event. And it seems the Bethmanns never had anything to do with Pomeroy, Washington. But the regional connection has fascinated people ever since.

There's no specific evidence that Grover Cleveland had any specific connection to the house in Pardee; the speculation is loose at best. As an article in the *Lewiston Tribune* noted, "Notably, there is no real documentation or evidence to prove Miner as the son of the president. Rumor is only a recipe containing a pinch of circumstance, a skosh of lore and perhaps a dash of Cleveland's reputation as somewhat indiscreet in his romantic entanglements."

Pardee has had some significant historical documentation. There's a book about the Pardee sector of the Clearwater Valley, the self-published *They Called This Canyon Home: the Bethmanns of Pardee, Idaho*, by Dick Southern and Susan Turner. (Turner, who lived in the valley and later in Spokane, Washington, collected the research materials, and Southern compiled it.) Southern noted recently that it does not "delve into the gossip and accusations."

He recounted, in an e-mail to this author:

I was more interested in what the Bethmanns accomplished historically, and their contribution to the development of the upper Clearwater. It's rather sad that people will/want to remember what grandma whispered about Frieda and Miner, than to acknowledge their accomplishments. After I published the manuscript, I did compile a list of the rumors, which changed by who was repeating the accusation. These, I found comical to the degree of being absurd, especially when there is no documentation of facts.

He added that "Emilie Bethmann was a woman of education, family wealth, a husband who died long ago, and who dictated to her family what information they could share with anyone. I believe she enjoyed the notoriety of the gossip as it kept other family information/secrets hidden."

You have to wonder what those might have been.

CHAPTER 7

The Ridgerunner

I f the mythology of being an Idahoan has any central core, any kernel of meaning, it probably begins with this: Idahoans are rugged individualists.

Idahoans love to celebrate the Old West, even as most people in the state now live in suburban-type environments. Idaho is getting ever more urban, but the notion of living far away from it all, out in the great wild, distant even from one's nearest neighbor, has never lost its appeal. It explains large parts of Idaho society and even its economy and politics.

While relatively few Idahoans ever have or will choose actually to live that way, some have and do. The author's wife, Linda Watkins, lived for a decade deep in Idaho's backcountry, working at guest ranches far away from paved roads, power lines, and telephones. Usually, though, there were at least one or two or three other people, and often more, in the area; it was not a complete hermit's existence.

There were and are real Idaho hermits, however. One of those Linda encountered from time to time, not far from one of her employment spots on the Salmon River, was Buckskin Bill. His nickname—legally, he was Sylvan Hart—did not mislead or disappoint the occasional visitors who made their way deep into Idaho's wilderness to see a legend. He was as tough and grizzled as he seemed to be. A native of Oklahoma, he picked out a remote spot on the Salmon River in the 1940s, built a small cabin, and stayed there until he died. He achieved some degree of fame, but never changed his mode of living. He became, in truth, a living legend.

Others like him were scattered, before and after, around the state. There was Cougar Dave (Dave Lewis) early in the twentieth century, near Big Creek; and Dugout Dick (Richard Zimmerman), who lived south of the city of Salmon in the middle of the century. But none of their relationships with the mainstream world was more fraught, more complex, or in many ways more mysterious— more completely emblematic of the myth of being an Idahoan— than that of "the Ridgerunner."

For more than a dozen years he was the unseen, speculated-about phantom of many of Idaho's most remote mountains. Then he fell briefly into the view of civilization, and he became even harder to understand.

The Ridgerunner, as he was most often called, was a mystery then and remains a puzzle still, since apparently no one knows what happened to him. He lived alone in the woods, for years at a time; interacted with other people sporadically and often unwillingly; and then simply vanished one spring day in 1964 into the Idaho wilderness.

We do not know for certain where he came from, and we cannot even be certain of his name.

He was wiry, short of stature, physically adept—able, for example, to undertake extremely long hikes under very poor conditions. He lived in the unsheltered open for weeks and months, in winter as well as summer, in some of the most challenging terrain on the continent. William Moreland, the name he was best known by and to which he answered for many years, was an Idaho individual.

He was born in 1900 (that year at least seems not to be in debate) in a rural area in Kentucky, although he once claimed Minnesota as a birthplace as well. His original name may not have been Moreland; he said in an early interview with the Forest Service that his birth name was W. C. Morrison. He told various stories about his father, whom he did not see from at least a very young age. He had a sister, about whom he said little; his mother, by the time the outside world caught up with him in Idaho, either had died many years before or had simply vanished from his life.

Moreland could read and write, though the extent of his education is unclear. He said he spent time in various reform schools in Kentucky and elsewhere; whether he graduated from high school, and if so where, is unknown. After that, he took off around the country. At first, he worked in lumber camps around the Great Lakes, and he said once, "I used to try to bum the chain gangs in Louisiana for food." Gradually he migrated toward the western states, working odd jobs, in manual labor and farm work, through his early adult years.

Long before the term had currency, Moreland lived off the grid. He resisted declaring a set address of any kind. He apparently never voted. He apparently never married.

He spent short stretches in prison, in Arizona for breaking into a grocery store, and in Arkansas in connection with a bank robbery, though there's reason to think he was wrongly accused in that case.

The onset of the Great Depression found him on the West Coast, mainly washing dishes in urban areas, hopping freight trains from one city to another. He was grabbed by law enforcement as a stowaway in Seattle and Tacoma around 1930. He took short-term jobs inland, in Pasco, Washington; in Bend, Oregon; and in Lewiston, Idaho.

In mid-1932—the date determined by Moreland's recollection that Franklin Roosevelt was running for president then—he came to Mountain Home, Idaho, and found work on a nearby ranch. Something happened there that made him quit civilization as far as he could. We have only scraps of information about what that was, but Moreland seems to have become obsessed with a girl who lived on the ranch. He was not accused of doing anything illegal, but the situation at the ranch and with people connected to it turned toxic.

So one day in the summer of 1932, William Moreland walked away. He headed north, up into the Danskin Mountains north of Mountain Home, and very slowly, over the course of more than a dozen years, he continued to work his way north. He would not revisit another city or town for more than thirteen years.

He may have visited the small mountain mining community of Atlanta a few weeks after leaving the ranch. From there Moreland hiked north to the Chamberlain Basin in what is now the Frank Church–River of No Return Wilderness. He would admit long after to trying to steal an airplane, an attempt that failed because he could not get it to start (and didn't in any event know how to fly it). A few years later found him in the Gibbonsville area not far from Salmon, and from there he crossed over the Bitterroot Mountains, northwest, into the Clearwater River basin.

By 1940 he was on the move around the North Clearwater River area, and in the ridges to its north, and in the St. Joe River basin on the other side of them. The few maps then existing for those places were thinly drafted, and Moreland probably did not have one; he was mapping the territory in his mind as he went. In this area his larger-scale wandering seemed to stop, and in his forties he seemed to have found a wilderness home in the vast and barely occupied backcountry forests of north-central Idaho. Year-round he often camped outdoors or set up a simple lean-to for modest shelter.

It was a hard life. He said later that in his early days in the Clearwater's North Fork basin he nearly starved: "I stumbled onto a cabin on Pot Mountain or I wouldn't be here now. All there was in the cabin was peanut butter. I found it in the food cache under the floor. I was so hungry I ate it with my fingers. It kept me alive."

But as he aged, he became a little less amenable to living completely out-of-doors. More than he had before, he was moving toward coming into contact with other people—or at least, toward the things they brought or built in the backcountry that could ease his life a little.

These mountainous forest lands were lightly occupied but not entirely empty of people. Several large organizations had claims of various sorts to much of that land, and small numbers of people were moving in. One of those organizations was the U.S. Forest Service, which operated national forests across much of the land where Moreland wandered—mainly the St. Joe National Forest to the north and the Clearwater National Forest to the south. Within these forests were ranger districts; ranger cabins were scattered throughout the country, and on the higher peaks the service operated forest fire lookout posts. Many of these outposts were connected by telephone, and in some cases by radio communications. These were not urban-style dwellings—typically they were basic and rustic—but they were functional, and usually provided a warm and safe place to stay.

Some of the timber companies had similar facilities, in smaller networks, and their lumber camps were often seasonal, ideal for a wanderer in the woods to get some occasional shelter. Moreland noticed all this.

He also observed the increasing encroachments of the timber companies, most notably the largest of them, Potlatch, which with the Weyerhaeuser Company owned immense tracts in northern Idaho and logged on national forest lands as well. The timber operators along with the Forest Service built roads, raised buildings, and began providing services in areas where humans never had developed settlements before. As they came, they began to encounter William Moreland.

The reports of him were fleeting at first: a strange, furtive man wandering the mountains on foot, connected to none of the new arrivals. They began to call him the Ridgerunner. In time, Moreland would accept that name for himself. He seemed to like it.

Before vanishing into the woods, Moreland had a history of thievery—a string of legal convictions for taking things that were not his.

In the woods, an old pioneer ethic prevailed that travelers could, as necessity arose, take what they needed. Did a wanderer need a place to stay and encounter an abandoned cabin? No problem: Just stay there. Hungry and thirsty? If food was stocked and something to drink was available, it was there to share. That ethic had gotten him imprisoned (and maybe sent to reform school) in urban society. In the backcountry the rules were more forgiving. To a point.

Various people in the backcountry were reporting in 1941 quick impressions of seeing someone—some unknown person they started to call the Ridgerunner. The word has its origins in the southern and Appalachian country, applying to moonshiners and others living remotely and outside the law.

In May 1942, Forest Service workers at the Round Top Ranger Station, deep in the St. Joe National Forest, returned from outdoors work to find that their radio was gone, along with a few other items. Not many days later, a Forest Service camp near Goat Ridge Lookout was relieved of several food cans, eggs, and items of clothing. A month later, in July, saw another theft from the Goat Ridge Lookout, where the items taken included a gun. More scattered burglaries were being reported at Forest Service outposts around the area.

The Forest Service was becoming annoyed.

The Ridgerunner, on a return visit to Round Top, was almost caught by a Forest Service worker, but his superior forest skills allowed him to slip away.

Moreland seemed to go underground the following winter, but in 1943 he surfaced again, once more taking food and equipment from Round Top, the first of about a half-dozen burglaries

The eastern mountaintops of the Bitterroot Mountains near Orofino, where the Ridgerunner spent much of his life.
RANDY STAPILUS

of backcountry cabins in the coming months. The topic of the Ridgerunner was becoming commonplace on the streets and in the homes around the smaller communities of north-central Idaho. For months, though, the Forest Service seemed at a loss to figure out where he was or where he was going. Without that information, they had a poor chance of catching him.

Not until March 1944 did a break emerge, by accident. Lewis Holt and Clyde Cole, two Forest Service workers sent to a remote area to evaluate efforts needed in the area that year, headed to the Flat Creek cabin, run by the agency, to stay overnight. No one was supposed to be there, but as they approached, they spotted a man inside, eating at the kitchen table.

They walked in and surprised the man, slight of build and in heavily worn clothes but—they remembered distinctly—with piercing eyes. A rifle stood against a wall. The man recovered quickly, said he was going out to feed his horse, and stalked through the front door and outside before Holt and Cole could much react.

They didn't even try to pursue him at first. They had a portable radio and used it to advise headquarters that they had encountered the Ridgerunner, and sought instructions.

An odd question arose: Did they have authority to arrest the Ridgerunner if they caught him? It turned out they did, but hours passed before a clear answer came through. Their pursuit of him was largely too late, but with a location and a general direction established, the Forest Service this time had a starting point for a search.

The forest supervisor gave the job of finding him to Moton Roarke, a woodsman whose experience in the backcountry almost equalled Moreland's. After growing up in a coal-mining town in Virginia, he headed west and had spent a quarter century in the forests by the time he was told to find Moreland.

The initial difficulty was finding Moreland's trail, but, working with another Forest Service veteran, Mick Durat, Roarke located what looked like the right trail. Day after day they patiently followed the trail across ridges and over dozens of miles. Finally they spotted him at a campfire, introduced themselves, and, without resistance, began the long trek back to headquarters to bring him in.

They brought the man before Holt and Cole—who promptly told them this was the wrong guy. Roarke had grabbed a man named Frank Davis, who in fact had stolen a few minor items but just as clearly was not the Ridgerunner.

The real article was once again keeping his head down. He left no trace through the summer and fall of 1944, and when winter came, Roarke was laid off, since his job was seasonal. But he stayed in the backcountry, trapping animals freelance on a state Fish and Game program, and kept his eyes open for any signs of the Ridgerunner.

One day he ran across them, and corralled a team who followed the thin traces over mountain and valley, through thick and thin snowpack. On February 9, 1945, they caught up with him in a canyon and trapped him next to a small tarpaulin he had set up. He was sitting near a campfire, opposite his few possessions—a rifle, the tarp, a sleeping bag, and some small cooking equipment.

Roarke walked up to him from behind. He said, "Hello."

The Ridgerunner turned and looked at him, and said, "I guess the dear rangers have been looking for me for a long time."

They had, but now the search was over. From that point, for the next two decades, William Moreland was a less obscure figure, if in many ways still a mysterious one.

When asked his name, he responded, "Bill Moreland." When asked for identification, he said he had none. Asked for a Social Security card, he said he didn't know what that was. Social Security had been around for about a decade at that point; Moreland never had signed up. He also had not signed up for the draft, a point that caused him some legal problems, though he was cleared of wrongdoing because he had headed back into the woods before the draft had begun, and he was unaware of it. Moreland was not even sure what the year was.

Moreland readily admitted to a long string of minor offenses, and a few larger ones. Charges were filed, and he was taken to the Nez Perce County jail in Lewiston, the first time he had been in a town in about thirteen years.

The U.S. attorney at the time, John Carver, said that most of the evidence was too thin and in some cases the law didn't fit well. Moreland was convicted of burglary, but given a suspended sentence and released. He quickly made his way back to the North Fork of the Clearwater, and for the next winter stayed with the owner of a river lodge and helped with hunting and upkeep. In the spring, as he had said he would, he took off again into the woods.

At times he lived as he had before, camping and staying on the move in the woods. With the end of World War II, however, timber cutting and production picked up in the Clearwater country, and increasing numbers of people made their way there. It was a less isolated place than it had been.

Moreland took occasional jobs working for timber companies, notably Potlatch Forest Industries, the largest timber firm in the area. He did not usually work directly on timber production, but rather on such jobs as scouting areas or preparing runs for the delivery of cut timber—more remote jobs that better suited his temperament.

Even that suited him only so well; unaccustomed to social situations, he easily got into conflicts with other people. He continued to live in remote cabins and didn't bother to cash the paychecks he received. At one point he made a company supervisor concerned when he started showing a lot of attention—and bestowing gifts, including paychecks—to the man's daughter.

One summer day in the early 1950s, after Moreland had been working there off and on for five years, company officials confronted Moreland at their offices at Headquarters—a small company town—and told him he would have to leave. Moreland said he was ready to head off into the woods again anyway, and appeared to do that. But not many nights later a Caterpillar D-8 bulldozer, one of the company's largest pieces of equipment, was spectacularly blown up with dynamite.

Moreland was assumed to have done it, and when he showed up at company headquarters a few days later, he was detained. In the trial that followed, at which Moreland was represented by future federal judge Ray McNichols, a jury declared him not guilty. He went back to the woods.

A couple of years after that, he was charged again, this time with assault with a deadly weapon. He was convicted, but served only part of a six-month sentence. He returned to the wilderness.

The Forest Service at first contented itself with simply keeping Moreland under loose observation, but change in management led to a harsher attitude in the summer of 1954. For two years Moreland stayed mostly in the Milk Creek area, and the feds kept watch. They brought him in on sundry charges, and Moreland continued to slip through the system.

Finally one of the charges stuck, sort of. Moreland was arrested again in October 1957 on charges of theft of Forest Service equipment—he had continued to break into Forest Service buildings from time to time—and was flown by helicopter to Lewiston and then locked up in Coeur d'Alene. For reasons that remain unclear, someone decided he should have a psychiatric evaluation. For that he was taken back south to Orofino, where a state mental hospital was located.

At the sanity hearing, no mental health professional testified; the only witness was a Forest Service official who had never met Moreland but still declared him "mentally deficient." That was enough for the judge, who committed the Ridgerunner to State Hospital North. He stayed there for five years, apparently cooperative and social. Once, in April 1959, he walked off from the hospital and spent a few days back at his Milk Creek shelter, but he soon returned to Orofino.

In August 1963, still at State Hospital North, he escaped out a window and headed back to the woods. A few people reported seeing him at various locations in the months that followed. The last of them was a logger named Jake Altmiller, whom Moreland had known for years. Around June 1964, he saw Moreland walking down a road near Pierce. Moreland told him, "I'm leaving for good." They shook hands, and Moreland turned and strolled down the road.

He has not been seen, or heard from, since.

CHAPTER 8

Noah Kellogg's Donkey

As you roll down I-90 through the Coeur d'Alene River valley, better known as the Silver Valley, you will see in between steep mountainsides an old mining region packed with local color, emerging from vivid stories reaching back a century and a half.

Some of this color grows out of the labor wars—and "war" is not too strong a word in this case—of the 1890s, with reverberations that have not settled yet. Some of it emerged out of the general hardness of life in the early mining area, and callous behavior and worse, such as the story that the ghosts of a group of Chinese workers, hanged underground at a mine development somewhere near Mullan, still haunt the area. The rooms above one of the venerated bars in the city of Wallace—a city lively enough that an old bordello is now one of the more popular museums in town—is said to be haunted too, though the alleged circumstances are vaguer. (Some local people admit those stories may have been invented as a marketing device.)

But the most popular legend of the Silver Valley, a tale happily shared with visitors from far and near, is an animal story.

It was long visible in a tourism sign just off I-90 near one of the Kellogg exits. The sign welcomed travelers to the place, with an unusual message: YOU ARE NOW NEAR KELLOGG. THE TOWN

WHICH WAS DISCOVERED BY A JACKASS—AND WHICH IS
INHABITED BY ITS DESCENDANTS.

Directions to the town's chamber of commerce follow.

At least the sign didn't point out that one of the early proposed names for the town actually was "Jackass." The name didn't
come out of thin air. It had some historical resonance. There is a
point to this odd sign, one rooted in the history—or at least legend—of the place. The story, repeated endlessly in the Silver Valley, formed the foundation of what would become Idaho's richest
mining region. It even lent its name to a popular local restaurant,
Noah's Canteen. It started with a grubstake.

The word "grubstake" sounds informal, and like many others
of the kind, this particular grubstake was. But unlike most, this one
was also important. It was important in the law and business of

This photograph of a long-standing road sign in Kellogg reflects the legend of
Noah Kellogg and his donkey.

the region, not to mention to many individuals, and in many other ways.

A grubstake is an investment, but often handled in an informal way, in many cases without cash. It might mean supplying a prospector for precious metals with supplies and equipment, just enough to get started, with the promise of sharing in the proceeds if the miner got lucky.

"An oral 'grubstake' contract performed on plaintiff's part will be enforced by a court of equity when established," a 1914 digest of Idaho Supreme Court rulings declared—and that had been the state of the law for decades. Idaho mining law was one of the earliest parts of territorial law to be developed, because mining was the first large-scale commercial activity in the territory, and many of the legal cases roiling through the courts in those days concerned mining claims. The mining laws for Idaho were passed by the legislature in 1864, the second year of the territory's existence, modeled on those of California and Nevada, which already had ample experience with gold rushes. The law of grubstakes was established early on, long before Noah Kellogg came into the Idaho Panhandle country.

Another unusual provision of the Idaho law, but shared with California and Nevada, was the allowance that when a person made claim on an outcropping that broke the surface of the ground, he could follow that metal deposit downward even at an angle, even outside the surface area on which he had staked a claim. Both provisions of that law would become vitally important to Noah Kellogg. And, presumably, to his donkey (often referred to as a "jackass") as well.

Kellogg's grave marker says he was born on December 18, 1831, but it does not say where that event happened. Kellogg's early decades generally have been lost to time. There's no record of where he was during, or if he was active in, the Civil War, which is a point prominent in the histories of many Americans of his generation. Kellogg is said to have become a carpenter by trade, but that may simply have meant he worked in odd-job construction. In the early 1880s, he was wandering around the West, a prospector and would-be laborer looking for the next big strike.

Ever since the gold rush in California in the late 1840s, the American West had been convulsed by a series of mining booms. Idaho had seen several, the northernmost at first being the gold rush at Pierce in 1862, the one that led shortly thereafter to creation of the Idaho territory. That find was soon followed by the boom in the town (now a ghost town) of Florence in the Salmon River basin, followed by others in Idaho City in 1863 (in the Boise River basin), in the Owyhee Mountains in 1868, and in the Wood River Valley in 1879. In the years after that, the frequent eruptions of mining booms and boomtowns were slowing, and the migrating force of prospectors was beginning to thin out. But they were not gone entirely.

Probably Noah Kellogg was among the mining migrants around the West, rootless fortune seekers bouncing around the mining hot spots in hopes of cashing in on the next big strike, a hope that always seemed just barely out of reach, almost like a series of scratch-off lottery tickets where the numbers all match but for one or two.

By the time he reached northern Idaho, Kellogg seemed familiar with the basics of mineral prospecting. But when he turned up along with a river of other eager prospectors in Murrayville, Idaho, in May 1884, having by that time reached the relatively advanced age of fifty-two, he had little to show for it, apparently not much more than the clothes he wore, and maybe a few cheap mining tools. But he was still searching for his main

Noah Kellogg discovered the massively rich silver deposit centered around the Kellogg area, for which Silver Valley was named.

chance, and he had some reason to think that in this new community he might find it.

Murrayville, an obscure place then and even more so now, was not part of what later would be called the Silver Valley. It was about thirty miles north of that area, in the northern reach of the Coeur d'Alene River basin. Today only a few people still live there. But mining in the region started in this spot.

Gold mining there was launched by Andrew Prichard (whose name would later attach to one of the smaller communities in the region), a veteran of the Missouri cavalry in the Civil War and an intensely religious man who envisioned an upright Christian community sustained by gold mining. (He seems not to have recognized the difficulty in putting those elements together.) Prichard searched around the Idaho Panhandle in the late 1870s, certain that precious metals could be found, supporting himself and his search by cutting timber through a contract with a company in Spokane. He did not focus, however, on what would become the wildly successful southern fork of the Coeur d'Alene River basin; instead, he explored around the north fork of the river, about thirty miles northward over the mountains, where some precious metals—but far fewer of them—were to be found.

In 1881, near what became known as Prichard Creek, Prichard found rich placers with value as high as $42 per pan. Smarter than some of his fellow prospectors, he tried to keep the find a secret, and managed to lock in his own claims, but other miners quickly appeared—including George Murray, namesake of the nearby community called Murrayville in 1884 and then, on order of the Post Office, Murray in 1885.

The Northern Pacific Railroad, interested in extending new lines around the region, publicized word of the new gold strike in February 1884. At a moment when mining rushes were relatively few, this one electrified the far-flung community of prospectors, and that spring they poured into town. Murray grew so fast that it grabbed the Shoshone County seat from Pierce, far to the south, which had held it since 1863.

Most of the miners were disappointed, however. The gold strike was significant but not enormous, and much of it played out quickly. Most of what was there was located around streams, and large dredging equipment was used to extract it. That left out the individual miner, who didn't have the resources to compete.

Noah Kellogg, arriving too late to do much useful prospecting on his own in the Murray area, for a couple of years fell back on carpentry, building flumes for the dredge mining projects. There are some indications that he was a more reliable and stable worker than some of the other migrants, but the work environment was neither reliable nor stable. His best employer was the Coeur d'Alene Water Supply Company, whose main business was building flumes through which water would be poured into the mines—necessary for various mining operations. Even that business, despite not being dependent on a single mine, had to scramble in chaotic economic conditions, and wound up issuing scrip (promises of payment) rather than actual cash or currency to its workers. When Kellogg and the other workers tried to spend it, they found they generally could get no better than 35 cents for each dollar.

Kellogg scoured around the mountains to the south of Murray, and then into the Coeur d'Alene River basin, tracking along the hillsides. The landscape looked right for a metal strike, he thought. But month after month went by, and he couldn't find it.

A few other small indicators of something bigger and better were appearing, though none had yet led to anything big. In September 1884, two brothers, True and Dennis Blake, filed a claim (which they called Silver Boy) on a tract roughly halfway between what is now Kellogg and Osburn, reporting a small silver find. Enough was there to work it to modest profit, and the brothers and their successors continued pulling small amounts of silver for decades. But not until the 1920s did a large successor company take over, rename the operation the Sunshine Mine, dig much deeper, and find a massive and highly profitable pit of silver buried there.

In the first half of 1885, there was little obvious clue that anything more than small deposits would ever be available in the drainage.

In the early summer of 1885, his funds depleted or probably gone entirely, Kellogg began to hit up people around Murray for a grubstake—enough money or supplies to carry on with his search. There were skeptics, but he could also make a case that northern Idaho wasn't yet done with precious metals. He persuaded two people involved with a range of business propositions, Dr. John Cooper and Origin Peck, to invest some supplies in his next search. The investment was not large, but it may indicate how limited Kellogg's own funds were. Some reports said the supplies were valued at (and maybe had cost) $18.75.

This was the important grubstake, and one of the few undebated points in all this was that the date the grubstake was finalized was August 1, 1885.

Kellogg took off from Murray this time newly provisioned with bacon, beans, flour, some small mining tools, and a burro named Bill—these things being the grubstake. That he actually did have a mule seems indisputable; there's likely no other way he realistically could have carried his equipment and supplies.

For the next two months he wandered the Coeur d'Alene basin region, gravitating toward the south fork of the river. Apparently taking a random walk, nearly aimless but hopeful, he reported finding nothing of value.

Returning to Murray, he looked up Cooper and Peck and persuaded them to restock his supplies of food, and he took off south once again. This time, with summer coming toward a close, he returned after only two weeks. Once again, he said he had found no precious metals. But according to the stories he told later, his burro had, about twenty miles south of Murray.

The Silver Valley, which is based around the south fork of the Coeur d'Alene, is often described as a single rich-metals mining area, but it is complex. There are six separate geological formations of interest to miners in this relatively small area (called the Prichard, the Burke, the Revett, the St. Regis, the Wallace, and the Striped Peak), and all but one of them produced metals of some value. The main ore metals there are galena, sphalerite, and tetrahedrite; the silver is found interspersed with them, mainly in the tetrahedrite. But not much of it was immediately obvious to the early travelers to the region. A piece of luck would be needed to scope out the region's true potential.

Little of value was found in the valley, close by the river; if anything was to be had, it would apparently have to present itself in higher elevations, in the mountains that rose up steeply on either side.

Kellogg and Bill were climbing the mountains above the south side of the river, close to what is now the city of Wardner, in an area called Milo Gulch. The hillside was open, relatively free of trees, and in the mountainous folds the geological landscape was relatively easy to evaluate. They were by now scoping out the area along with two other prospectors Kellogg had met along the way, men named O'Rourke and Sullivan. All of them were interested in the prospects of the area but failing to come across any specific findings of metal.

As Kellogg told the story, he left the burro alone for a time as he wandered around Milo Gulch, and lost track of it. He called after it, and when he found Bill, the animal was braying and standing over a bright shining metal, almost lighting his way to what would become a fabulous precious metal find.

The donkey discovery story has been commemorated in image and poem and even in the special striking of coins, such as this one, minted by the Metal Arts Company of New York as part of the 1981 Bunker Hill Company Silver Medallion Series.

An alternate version of the story reflects differently, though not especially better, on Kellogg and the donkey: Bill kept wandering off, Kellogg had to chase it down, and finally he got angry enough to pick up a rock to throw it at the animal. The rock, the story has it, was made of galena.

There is a variation on the legend: that Noah's deceased brother Milo began appearing to him (and, apparently, to Bill the donkey) while he was exploring for mining opportunities along the south fork, and led him up the hill where the galena deposit was found.

The initial find, supposedly by Bill, wasn't much. It apparently contained nothing more than quartzite with a surface stained by iron, with small bits of galena on top.

The galena was nonetheless enough to get his attention. Galena is the most important form of iron ore, and more important, is a key source of silver—which is what it looks like on the surface. Kellogg and his prospecting friends dug around the area and began to find the goods.

When he returned to Murray on August 27, he told Cooper and Peck he had found reason for encouragement, though apparently he didn't let on much more. Once he got to the courthouse, he filed paperwork—with himself as a witness—on a personal claim at Milo Gulch. And he made moves, quietly and fast, to work it. He persuaded Cooper and Peck to give him yet another grubstake, and only two days after his return to Murray, he headed south again to the site where he'd spotted the quartzite.

On September 13, he came back, reported that he had not found what he hoped for, gave the pack jackass and the tools back to Cooper and Peck, and offered to end the grubstake deal with them. But as was so often the case, word did not stay quiet. On his last journey south, other prospectors noticed unusual behavior on Kellogg's part, and Kellogg made surreptitious deals with several of them toward developing the area—on which he already had an original claim.

Cooper and Peck, who under the grubstake agreement were properly owed a large share of any valuable finds, quickly figured out the truth and filed a lawsuit. A district judge granted the two of them partial rights to Kellogg's find. From there the story became immensely more complex and mired in the details of mining law, and many of the relevant facts have been contested or cloudy.

By one account, "Since Kellogg did not know the value of the ore he found, he showed some of the iron-stained galena to Philip O'Rourke, a former Leadville miner then being grubstaked by Jacob Goetz, who recognized it as valuable ore. The two then located the Bunker Hill claim in O'Rourke's name. On October 2, Cornelius Sullivan, a friend of O'Rourke, located the Sullivan claim across the gulch, and soon all the adjacent ground was taken up."

Other interests soon also made their way into the development, which came to be named mainly for the hillside, Bunker Hill; for some years it was called the Bunker Hill and Sullivan mine.

Whatever the sometimes fuzzy details surrounding its origins, the history of the Bunker Hill mine in the generations since has been legendary. Over the next century more than thirty-five million tons of ore, including vast amounts of silver, were mined there. The launching of the Bunker Hill mine also led to the digging of numerous other mines around what became famously known as the Silver Valley. That mining district has been ranked among the top ten mining districts in the world for value of metals extracted.

Kellogg personally was not one of the prime beneficiaries of the one of the most prosperous mining districts in the United States. He may have staked out the original location for the mining activity, but he had no resources to throw at developing it—and for the kind of underground mines needed to extract the silver, massive resources would be needed. He sold at first some, and then in 1887 practically all, of his interest in the property to a Portland businessman and investor named Simeon G. Reed. Reed developed the property for five years but soon flipped it, recognizing the high cost involved in processing the ore pulled out in this area. The next owner was a tough and well-financed syndicate from San Francisco, which adopted a harder line with labor policy that in turn led to the violent and bloody labor wars in the Silver Valley in the 1890s.

Kellogg did bequeath his name to a nearby community, Kellogg, which was located about a dozen miles from the Bunker Hill area but became the largest city in the Silver Valley. He lived to age seventy-two, dying on March 17, 1903. He is buried at Kellogg.

Kellogg has a long history as a mining town, and some of that activity still is underway. Kellogg still has a local of the United Steelworkers (number 5114); and mining jobs, which pay well, have increased gradually in the new century. Still, with the overall decline of mining in the Silver Valley, it has shifted focus in recent years. Massive mining-related pollution in the area led to designation in the late twentieth century of a large Superfund site in the area, but a great deal of that waste has been cleaned away.

In the last couple of decades, more emphasis has been placed on Kellogg's potential for tourism. Its promoters have tried rechristening it as a Bavarian village. Large condo developments, on the mountainside and down in the valley, have emerged in the new century. A large ski area has been developed in the mountains high above, with a spectacular gondola connecting it with the downtown district.

And yet for many years people driving by would see the sign saying: THIS IS THE TOWN FOUNDED BY A JACKASS AND INHABITED BY ITS DESCENDANTS.

There is also a silver "round" coin struck in the 1981 Bunker Hill Company Silver Medallion Series. The coins—about thirty thousand of them were struck—include some actual silver.

The historical record is completely silent, after his final return to the county seat of Murray, on what became of Bill.

CHAPTER 9

The Corridor Killings

Northern Idaho is mainly forested wild land, all mountainous save for a few small and scattered prairies. It is thinly dotted with traces of human civilization, linked with thinner strings of road.

These strings are few. Today there is a major, thick string to the north running east and west, called I-90, tracking roughly the path of the very old Mullen Trail of the mid-1800s. About a hundred miles south there's another string—thinner, more winding, and less used than the other—called Highway 12, which was not fully connected east and west or in any sense completed until the early 1960s. South of them for more than two hundred miles there are no paved roads—no roads at all that most motor vehicles can easily travel during any time of year—that fully connect Idaho east and west. The country is too mountainous, too difficult to build through, too remote, too lightly populated.

But long ago, there was another rough transportation route running east and west through the Idaho Panhandle, slicing through this rough country, south of today's Highway 12. It was almost ancient by Idaho standards; it was known to the people who did live there as the best way to get from Washington Territory to

Montana Territory. It was not really a road; more a trail. But it was all they had.

Native Americans used much of it for hundreds of years when they sought to cross the Bitterroot Mountains. It was a known route—known to the people who did travel the interior of the Northwest—not long after the Lewis and Clark days. In 1835, a missionary named Samuel Parker walked the trail, from east to west, and described some of what he saw then, in one of the earliest descriptions of what is now Idaho:

> Can this section of the country ever be inhabited, unless these mountains shall be brought low and these prairies exalted? But they may be designed to perpetuate a supply of lumber for the widespread prairies, or they may be mines of treasures which when wrought will need those forests for fuel and these rushing streams for power.

But none of that would happen, not around that trail.

Adventurous travelers still traverse it. Some try it with especially hardy motor vehicles (this is a rough and uncertain drive at best); others hike it, or travel on horseback. If it can be considered an actual road, it may be—at nearly one hundred twenty miles in length—the longest single unpaved road, with no services or even residences along it, in the contiguous forty-eight states. It snakes through a narrow pass between two massive wilderness areas, the Frank Church–River of No Return to the south and the Selway-Bitterroot to the north. Save for the road itself, and a few campgrounds along the way, it looks as wild today as the wilderness areas do, and as wild as it did two centuries ago.

The Idahoans of early days did not have a name for it. Today, though it is found only on certain specialized kinds of maps, it does have a name, a couple in fact. Its more or less official name is the Nez Perce Trail Road, but it is better known among longtime Idahoans as the Magruder Corridor.

From Lewiston, for a traveler headed to Montana, the first portion was a well-established lowlands road, leading southeast toward the prairie towns—then just in their earliest days past birth—around what is now Grangeville. From there you would drive farther southeast, hugging the banks of the south fork of the Red River, until at its easternmost point you break off and head east.

From that point you head up and down, through forests and over and along Poet Creek and Bargamin Creek. About thirty-five miles out, there's a fantastic view of the northern stretch of the Frank Church–River of No Return Wilderness. The trail runs east, uphill, to the headwaters of the Selway River, and finally upward of seven thousand feet high in places to the pass over the Bitterroot Mountains, Nez Perce Pass, about eighty-seven miles northeast of the Red River. Beyond that, in Montana, the trail continues down the mountains into the valley south of Darby.

About fifty miles along this route, the traveler will encounter a Forest Service sign. It is short and cryptic, and it refers to a murder. It is the lone point along the way that helps explain, though not clearly, how this route got the common name of the Magruder Corridor.

In 1862, when Lloyd Magruder arrived from California in Lewiston with his wife and children, he had already marked himself as something uncommon.

At that moment, Lewiston was a busy if brand-new small town, but in common with most frontier communities, most of the people there were men who were either single or at least unaccompanied by family. Many of them were eager, intense, and ambitious, and grasping as well; there was no lack of sharps and criminals among their number.

Magruder was nothing like this. Like other recent arrivals, he had spotted opportunity and hoped to make a living from it, but his plan involved establishing himself along with his family in a new community. Had he lived longer, he might have become a mayor or a state legislator; he was a pillar-of-the-community type in the kind of community that saw few of them in those days. He had been involved in politics before; a native of Maryland with strong ties to the South, he was a firm Democrat and no fan of the Lincoln administration. The mining areas of much of the West were Democratic, which meant Magruder was flowing with the local political tide. He had been elected clerk of Yuba County, California, and now in Lewiston he was making friends as well. In the summer of 1862, friends were inquiring of him whether he would be interested in standing for election as the territorial delegate to Congress—as a Democrat of course. He probably had some interest.

But Magruder was otherwise occupied.

He was not a miner, as were some of the newcomers—those who planned to go on to the new goldfields at Pierce and Oro Fino—he instead planned to provide goods and services for them.

Lewiston was a base and supply camp for many of the miners, and Magruder opened a business to serve them.

By the time Magruder got there with family in tow, the Pierce and Oro Fino diggings already were beginning to slip, the beginning of what would be a steep decline that almost eliminated those towns and erased a large slice of Lewiston's commerce in the process.

Magruder was unable easily to unearth his stakes yet again and move, so he rewrote his business plan. Fortunately, options were available. A new, midsized metals rush was just then blooming over the Bitterroots in Montana, near the new town of Bannack. It was located a vast distance from any available supplier of needed goods, and the closest practical supply route ran from the Pacific coast up through Lewiston, and then over the mountains on a trail known mainly to Native Americans and trappers.

It was a rough way to ship goods, but in the spring of 1863, Magruder, seeing his customer base moving east, made plans to supply it with the basics: sundries, food, whiskey, flour, and other goods. The only business advantage would be that the prices paid for these things, in those heavily inflationary mining communities, would be high. But Magruder figured he could make it work.

The ideal departure time would have been the earlier part of summer, no later than early July, but Magruder needed time to collect his supplies and round up a pack train. He hired about two dozen packers and about sixty mules to travel the couple hundred miles, over mountains and rivers, to the east. Not until early August were they ready to move.

It was a significant opening step in developing the commerce of Lewiston with points farther east, and Magruder's efforts were watched closely. Not least of the watchers was one of Magruder's friends, a stoutly built but highly energized man named Hill Beachey, who owned and ran a new Lewiston hotel called the Luna House. The night before the departure, Beachey slept poorly; he was beset by nightmares, dreams about the terrors of the wilderness that awaited Magruder—and specifically, clear dreams that Magruder would be killed, and his money stolen, somewhere along the way.

Not until days later, after the train had left, would he tell anyone about the dreams. But when Magruder made ready to depart, Beachey handed him a rifle, insisted that he take it—Magruder declined at first—and warned him to exercise great care and caution. Magruder thought he was overreacting, but finally accepted the rifle.

The first steps along the way went smoothly enough; in the opening days of the trip, he was able to stop at small, already developing settlements, where he could also transact some business. The first was Fort Lapwai, a center of Nez Perce population, where the army had an outpost; the commander there was a friend, and they had dinner together. He traded with some of the Nez Perce a little farther along the way, and then stopped at Elk City, a tiny and brand-new mining encampment.

That was the last settlement before Montana. Heading east from Elk City, he and the train managed about ten to fifteen miles a day, climbing sometimes steep hills, cutting or removing trees,

The first recorded mass murder in Idaho took place along this remote trail in the north-central Idaho mountains.

SAMUEL CHOU

crossing creeks. The late-summer weather was helping, but that wouldn't last long. They had no time to waste.

When he arrived in Bannack, Magruder's initial optimism about his commercial prospects faded. His history with gold rushes was repeating itself: Once again, he was coming just behind the curve. The rush near Bannack was still on, but it was deflating, and the town was already starting to lose population.

His bigger problem with Bannack, though, was with the new sheriff in town. He was an old acquaintance from Lewiston, but not a favorable one, and Magruder likely hadn't known he was there. Henry Plummer was also an ex-Californian, but he arrived in Lewiston with the goal of making money any which way he could; Magruder-style scruples were not in his makeup. Plummer too had been an elected official, a town marshal, but he had been imprisoned at San Quentin for killing two men without cause. Arriving in Lewiston for a fresh start, he stayed at the Luna House, and there Magruder and Beachey got a good sense of his character, and of the criminal element—robbers, rustlers, and the like—in his social circle. When he left town for an uncertain future, the Lewiston establishment, including Magruder, was glad to see the back-side of his horse.

Now he was well established at Bannack, working both sides of the law, and Magruder soon slipped out of town. He had heard that Virginia City was now the hot mining location, and he made his way there. This time he got lucky, unloading his supplies there to eager miners at high prices.

The detour meant more days stuck in Montana, however, and Magruder now had to return home as fast as he could, before the snows fell over the Bitterroots. That was becoming problematic by this point, around mid-September, and many of the people in his summer crew now planned to stay on the east side of the mountains through the winter. In late September, he decided to head back with a much smaller entourage, just a few horses and people—and his money. Late in the month he turned back toward Lewiston with Charles Allen, who had been the chief of his pack train.

He was bringing with him about $18,000, largely in the form of gold dust. Magruder was not inclined toward great caution, but he did recognize that if word got out that two men were traveling that nearly two-hundred-mile wilderness trail alone, with such a valuable and easily robbed haul, they would present an irresistible target.

Magruder and Allen had difficulty finding anyone in Virginia City to go with them, to bulk up the traveling party. So he made an understandable mistake: He stopped in Bannack to find additional help.

What he came up with was three half-bright ne'er-do-wells named Christopher Lower, James Romain, and David Renton. At the last moment, a fourth addition, an inexperienced and naive teenager named Billy Page, who was looking to return to his former home in Walla Walla, joined the group. Finally three more were added: two brothers named Chalmers and another packer named Bill Phillips, who wanted to travel to Lewiston.

Magruder, Allen, and the Bannack contingent walked out of Bannack on October 3, just as snow was about to hit the mountains. Some of them would never see civilization again.

They made excellent time at first, surmounting Nez Perce Pass within a week, and saw no one along the trail other than a couple of travelers on horseback who were headed the other way, into Montana. Soon after crossing into Idaho, Lower called Page to the side and brought him into the picture. Page had been unaware of why Magruder and Allen wanted their company, other than maybe for personal protection. Lower told him the Lewiston businesspeople were carrying $18,000 in gold. But, he added, they wouldn't be carrying it for long. In fact, they wouldn't be traveling much farther down the trail. Lower, Renton, and Romain were planning to see to that.

He didn't explain how he or the others knew about Magruder's money. And he warned Page: "If you value your life, stay alert but stay quiet."

The other travelers noticed that in the next few days Page seemed jumpy, but no one knew why. He kept his mouth shut.

A little over a week into the trip west, the weather was still holding up, barely. Magruder decided to stop for the night at a sheltered location between a cliff and a shallow ravine. Allen was skeptical, warning of probable snow the next day, but he was overruled; most of the others thought this would be a good location. Observing the limited opportunities at this spot for escape by their targets, Lower, Renton, and Romain in particular thought so.

After dinner, the group sat up talking before the campfire; most of them turned in after dark. Magruder decided to take the first shift keeping watch. Lower stayed up talking with him, and then Renton, who said he had been trying to get to sleep, joined them. The night was quiet, the conversation kept low.

The fire began to wear down, and Renton said he would chop some more wood for it. Lower reached over and grabbed the group's ax, and said he'd join him. But there would be no more woodcutting tonight.

As Lower began to step away from the campfire, he swung around and smashed the flat metal of the ax against the back of Magruder's skull. The force of the blow pitched him directly into the campfire. Renton grabbed the ax from Lower and immediately smacked Magruder again on the head, to make sure he was gone.

Romain, who may or may not have been sleeping, was alert by now, and the three of them walked over to a shocked Page.

Renton said, "You awake?"

Page could only nod; no words would come.

"Stay there."

Page had left on a simple journey to return to his home to the west, and now he was in the middle of a mass murder.

Because at this point it did become mass. The Chalmers brothers were fast asleep, and Romain and Renton quickly killed each of them with the ax. They turned and walked back to near where Page was, but off to the side. The ax then fell—literally—on Phillips.

One more kill remained. Allen, the train master who had been predicting a snowfall, had set up his tent rather than sleep in the open on a bedroll like the others. The close quarters with the tent material made the ax a poor weapon choice this time, so Renton returned to his bedroll and pulled out his shotgun. He opened the flap of Allen's tent, pointed the firearm inside, and fired. Half of Allen's head was blown away.

Page was in shock. He may have thought he was next. He was not, for one reason: He was the only traveler of the four remaining who knew the route back to Lewiston and beyond. None of the others ever had been that way.

Romain stood next to him and tried to calm him. "You're all atremble," he said. Nothing to worry about, he added; the rough stuff was over.

They still had cleanup to do. The killers had not done a lot by way of preparation, but one thing Renton did back in Bannack was to buy moccasins, four pairs of them, and the killers put them on, tromping around the camp. They would try to use the footprints, should they ever be seen, to pin the killings on Indians. The bodies were dragged away and rolled down into the ravine. Then the four remaining travelers trudged west, toward Lewiston.

It was not an easy trip. Allen's concerns about the weather proved right, and in the first week of October, rain and then snow poured down on them, as if in punishment for what had happened. They had to avoid civilization as best they could, bypassing the few small settlements on the way and sneaking back into Lewiston.

They had to go there because it was the only way west, and the killers' destination was the Pacific coast—Portland maybe, or the Puget Sound, or maybe San Francisco; their intentions probably were scrambled at this point. Renton had the idea of hiring a boat to run them down the Snake River, to get at least somewhere close to its merger with the Columbia River. Somewhere far away from the killing fields. But he could find no boats headed that way soon. Then Renton told Lower to find a stage for hire—or, if nothing else, one simply headed west. Lower went to the logical place to find one, and in doing that made a fatal mistake.

He walked into the stage office at the Luna Hotel, and there was spotted by the hotel's owner, Hill Beachey. Beachey was already concerned that his friend Magruder was overdue back from Montana. Now here was an agitated man who obviously had spent plenty of time in the elements, seemed to have plenty of money, and wanted four tickets—to include three people who were yet unseen—to get him away from town, as far west and as fast as possible. In trying to cover his backstory, Lower tripped over his words and contradicted himself several times; he was lying, repeatedly. The pieces added up in Beachey's mind.

Lower bought the tickets eventually, but the stage wasn't set to leave until the next morning. Beachey tried to get the Nez Perce County sheriff to keep the stage from leaving for Walla Walla, but he was unconvinced, and the stage left with the four travelers. Beachey pursued the case, though, asking people in town about the four, and finally did convince the sheriff to appoint him a deputy and let him go after the stage.

Calculating the stage's route and the group's probable direction, Beachey rode a horse as fast as he could to Portland. He was right in his estimates but not quite fast enough to get there in time; just before he arrived, a ship left Portland with the three killers and Page, headed south to San Francisco.

He turned for help to local Portland police, who sent a fast messenger south to San Francisco, and there police were able to arrest the four as they left their ship—and send them all back to Lewiston.

The scene turned ugly once they arrived; a lynch mob wanted to dispense rough justice right away. Instead, Page delivered compelling evidence against the other three, and supplied many of the details of what had happened, allowing for trial testimony that told that community what had happened. Lower, Romain, and Renton were convicted and hanged in Lewiston in March of 1864.

None of it was enough to keep Beachey in town. He was already preparing to leave Lewiston; he would migrate south to Nevada, where he died a few years later. But before that, just two months after the hangings, he decided to take a hike.

He and a few other Lewistonians took off to the southeast, and then west, along the thin trail Magruder had used the year before. They looked carefully for evidence and followed closely the evidence of Page's testimony indicating locations of various events. And finally they found the site: the bodies and personal items from the Magruder group. He put down a marker to show the spot.

That marker is long gone. Many, many years later, the Forest Service put up a sign in at least the same general place. And there's no clear knowing how many of the periodic travelers of the Magruder Corridor have any idea of the legacy on the ground under their feet.

CHAPTER 10

UFO Highway

An Idahoan was the person most directly responsible for coining the term "flying saucer," because that was similar to the shape of what he claimed he saw. Ironically, he didn't mean to suggest that it was extraterrestrial in nature. His guess was that it was something new developed by the American military.

Ken Arnold was a Boise-based pilot operating a small air service business. He was flying around the Northwest in his single-engine CallAir A-2 on June 24, 1947, when he saw what he thought were flying objects in the skies over the mountains in Oregon. He told a reporter at the Pendleton *East Oregonian* about it, and in the June 25 edition, the paper in turn published his claims.

Arnold, an experienced pilot who was not known for wild claims, said he thought he saw a V formation of nine objects flying at about seventeen hundred miles per hour. They seemed to be blue and glowing, like nothing he was accustomed to seeing in nature.

The Pendleton paper didn't use the term "flying saucer," but as Arnold's sighting was mentioned in the weeks to come in one place after another, the term was quickly coined and caught on. That was when the idea of flying saucers took off—as did a nationwide wave of sightings. Reports of extraterrestrial activity at Roswell, New

Mexico, soon thereafter locked in the nationwide interest in . . . whatever it was.

Some of the highest-placed comments about them came from one of Idaho's U.S. senators at the time, Glen Taylor. Taylor didn't necessarily think they were extraterrestrial in origin—though he said he almost hoped they were, and would help us humans settle some of our problems—but he suggested that whatever the explanation, "they can't be simply laughed off." If they were military in origin, what did it mean if they were American—or if they were Soviet? And, he said, "Even if it is only a psychological phenomenon, it is a sign of what the world is coming to. . . . If we don't ease the tensions, the whole world will be full of psychological cases and eventually turn into a global nuthouse."

People the world over have reported seeing odd things in the sky through most of recorded history. But interest in the idea of extraterrestrial beings, and some concrete idea of what they and their craft might look like, only began to take shape in the popular imagination well into the twentieth century. It coalesced, finally, when Idaho's Arnold made his declaration of seeing . . . something.

But Idaho has a significant UFO connection, in addition to claiming the reporter of the first major sighting, unusual in the annals of the field. It is home to what some people have called, and still call, the UFO Highway.

Idaho is of course hardly unique in its reports of UFOs. Neighboring Washington has it beat statistically for sheer numbers of reports. And nearby McMinnville, Oregon, holds an annual summer street festival celebrating UFOs (and related phenomena) based on a 1950 sighting, captured in a newspaper-published picture, allegedly showing a UFO just outside of town.

The National UFO Reporting Center said that, after crunching numbers on reported sightings, Idaho ranked tenth among the fifty states for most observations.

And Idaho has some of the most unusual and striking UFO sightings reported anywhere in the country. One of the first incidents to be considered serious enough to generate a formal inquiry came near Twin Falls only a couple of months after Arnold's sighting, on August 13, 1947. A local farmer and his sons were fishing at the Snake River Canyon north of town around midday when they spotted what they described as a "hat shaped"—it wasn't clear what sort of hat was meant—flying object, about twenty feet wide and colored blue. They thought it was about three hundred feet from where they were (presumably unsuccessfully) trying to attract fish; trees and other plants thrashed about, though it didn't seem to generate much breeze. How close a look they could have gotten is unclear, since they said it traveled at about a thousand miles an hour. Later that same day, a Twin Falls County commissioner said he saw something odd in the sky about thirty miles to the south at Salmon Falls Creek Reservoir. The FBI and the Air Force both looked into the claims, but ended their review with no conclusive results.

Many other places around Idaho have been host to reported incidents, but none compares with a patch of territory in the southeast sector of the state. The "UFO Highway" is the region between Pocatello and Soda Springs, along Highway 30 (including in part I-15), especially around the smaller communities of McCammon and Lava Hot Springs. It is in most respects an unremarkable area; there's no obvious reason that intelligent beings of either terrestrial origin or otherwise would take special notice of it.

The area in question is southeast of the city of Pocatello. In the mountains of that area, the Portneuf River emerges along the east side of the Fort Hall Indian Reservation (home to the Bannock and Shoshone tribes), northeast of Blackfoot. The river twists in a generally southern direction past the old ghost town of Chesterfield, then farther south and downhill to the geothermal community of Lava Hot Springs. From there it turns to the right, headed downhill and northwest along the valley toward the small city of McCammon, and from there roughly north to Pocatello before it merges a few miles beyond with the Snake River. Interstate 15 runs parallel to the river from Pocatello to McCammon. The river then diverges to the southeast, and starting at I-15 at McCammon on to Lava Hot Springs, the river is paralleled by Highway 30.

Most of this area is near-desert farm- and ranchland very much like that found across southern Idaho. The community of Lava Hot Springs is a little different, for the reasons its name suggests. It never has developed a large national visibility, but regionally it is well known for its naturally hot swimming pools and options for therapy. As one tourist brochure said, "Long before settlers discovered the natural, odor-free mineral waters in this quiet valley, the Bannock and Shoshone Indian Tribes gathered here to bathe, rest, and worship. For centuries, the Indians paid tribute to the Great Spirit for the curative powers of these springs and set the area aside as a neutral ground to be shared in peace by all tribes."

White settlers in the area soon discovered the hot springs and pools for themselves, and Lava Hot Springs has become a small recreation and resort community. Since 1911 the state of Idaho has run them as an unusual for-profit venture. Maybe the unusual geothermal properties of the area attracted some visitors from even further afar . . .

The Highway 30 region, centered perhaps around Lava, has, after all, had a large collection of UFO sightings. The most extensive of these reports involved an unusual collection of witnesses: police officers.

The case was reported in detail in a short 2017 book called *Smokey and the UFO,* by Tim Anderson, who is himself a former law enforcement dispatcher. He didn't specify when the events occurred, but other reports set the time period at the mid- to late 1970s. But he described the region from McCammon to Soda Springs as a hot spot for UFO sightings, and notably by law enforcement. Anderson wrote:

> When a police officer goes on the record as having spotted a UFO, it usually creates quite a stir. These are trained observers and expected to be more credible than most people who say they've seen something strange in the sky. What, then, should be expected when not just one, but four respected police officers step forward and announce they have seen not one but several UFOs at various times during their law enforcement careers?

One of the first of these reports came from Idaho State Police corporal Dennis Abrams, one night when he was on patrol near Soda

Springs. He recalled the time as about two in the morning when, off in the distance, over a mountain in an area called Wood Canyon, a light shone from some indeterminate source. He speculated that it might be a plane seeking a landing place; landing strips were in limited supply in the area. Then, briefly, the light flickered brightly.

He started uphill along the rugged roads to see if anyone needed assistance, if some kind of accident had happened. The roads rapidly became very rough, suitable mainly for backcountry vehicles, and he stopped and called for county law enforcement and emergency help. With vehicles built for rougher roads, they eventually made their way past him.

Heading back downhill, Abrams rounded a bend then, and then, he said, "I suddenly saw this luminous object off to my right. It was so close, I think I could have hit it with a rock. It was hovering just over the treetops."

Abrams said he was thrown by what he had seen, and got on his patrol unit's radio and described what he was seeing. He considered fleeing but instead sat there, inside the car, staring at the object. After about five minutes, he said, it flew directly upward and disappeared.*

That same night, wrote Anderson, another state police officer, Corporal E. H. "Chris" Christensen, was on patrol about twenty miles to the northwest, close to McCammon. He was listening to

---

*A summary of this was included in the National UFO Reporting Center recordings, 1974 to 1989, online at https://archive.org/stream/NationalUfoReportingCenterRecordings1974To1989/ NuforcDirectory_djvu.txt. It reports: "Idaho State Police Trooper Dennis Abrams Encounter of December 8, 1976 at Soda Springs, ID. This case was covered in a 1977 issue of International UFO Reporter." Another UFO tracking site, thecid.com, reported, "Unusual objects were sighted, that had unconventional appearance and performance. Two objects were observed by more than one male witness, one of them an experienced observer."

Numerous accounts of UFO sightings have been reported along Highway 30 in southeastern Idaho.

Abrams's radio reports and decided to help (and maybe check it out for himself). A few seconds after he started on his way, he spotted a luminous object in the sky headed his way. It was very bright and shaped like a football; it headed over him and back farther to the northeast, and beyond the horizon. Christensen said it must have shot from Abrams's location twenty miles away to his in a matter of seconds.

Because the incidents popped up in police records, word soon spread to local news organizations; newspapers and local television stations began reporting them. A business owner in Soda Springs chimed in to say he thought he had seen something too.

Six months later, Christensen said, he had another UFO experience. He was nearing the intersection of I-15 and Highway 30, a little uphill from the small town of McCammon—not too far from where he'd reported his earlier sighting. Construction work was underway in the area (it seems to be a frequent location for roadwork), and Christensen had a specific mission there, to make sure all equipment and supplies were cleared away from the road, to keep an accident from happening.

He was on the interstate's off-ramp, and beginning to approach the top of it, when something large and bright appeared in the construction area nearby. He saw a big, gray object sitting near the construction equipment. As he paused to take in the unexpected item in the field, strobe lights popped on, and the object lifted fast, so fast he could barely follow it, into the night sky. He may have been the lone observer of that incident. But next time around, he would have a co-witness with him.

Once again, the time was early in the morning, and close by I-15 near Highway 30. Christensen was parked and talking with a local deputy sheriff who was also on patrol; each was driving a vehicle from his agency. In mid-conversation they looked up, and both saw a distant light in the sky that seemed to be "dancing." They had binoculars, and used them to get a better look. The bright object actually seemed to be shaped somewhat like a saucer. It continued bouncing around in the sky, moving at what the officers thought was fantastic speed, for five, six, maybe as long as ten minutes. And then it vanished.

This sighting did not, at the time, result in a formal report by the officers.

But a fourth, months later and shortly after Christmas, did, because Christensen thought this time his vehicle was at risk. This incident also turned up in local newspaper accounts.

Once again he was in the McCammon area, once again well past midnight, and again with another law officer. After taking care of some work there, they decided to look for a hot coffee in Lava Hot Springs. The officers, in their respective cars, drove east of McCammon on Highway 30 and there encountered a bright light; he compared it to the headlight of a train bearing down a track. Christensen braked and pulled over to the side of the road; the other officer did the same.

The light passed and then turned fainter. The officers caught their breath, slowly returned to their cars, and drove the few remaining miles into Lava Hot Springs. A newspaper report said that several residents of the city also said they had seen some unusual lights late that night.

Sometime later, after the report went public, Christensen agreed with the view that what the officers saw might have been the planet Venus. He was hoping, he said, to get the light of attention off himself and let the whole thing go. Anderson reported later, however, that the officer later said that what he saw clearly was not Venus. The distant planet, he said, would not have forced him off the highway.

Still another law enforcement encounter, in Anderson's account, was reported by John Messinese, a deputy sheriff in

Bannock County with about fifteen years of law enforcement experience. After going to work in Bannock County, he said he saw UFOs, or something like them, on three different occasions. He spotted one at Arimo, in southern Bannock County southwest of Lava Hot Springs. This was in the form of a light in the sky making odd, erratic movements; he said that he observed it with another officer from his department present. Messinese said he saw another one night while ticketing a driver, and talking to him. He was quoted by Anderson: "I said to the guy, 'Hey, do you see that?' It was pretty obvious from the look on his face that he did." What they saw, Messinese reported, was something like one of Christensen's lights, something that looked roughly like a flying saucer.

His other experience happened after midnight, just following New Year's Eve, after the winding down of a holiday party in Lava Hot Springs. Messinese was headed out from Lava when he spotted a car that had broken down on the road. Three boys were inside, and he knew them because they were sons of a local law officer. He said he would give them a ride back home to Lava Hot Springs.

En route, he saw a bright light, possibly a star, that looked as if it was following his car. He called in to his dispatcher, joking that he might have spotted a UFO. Then the light seemed a little nearer, and it shifted its location, to the side, and to the front.

When he reached the boys' home, the other law officer joined him, and they looked up between a couple of low mountain peaks. The light seemed to have positioned itself there. The group watched it for several minutes. They looked at it through binoculars and through a rifle scope. All seemed to be still. For a time.

Finally, as the early-morning hours wore on, Messinese decided to get back on the road and head up Highway 30 toward McCammon and I-15, to return back to his home base of Pocatello. When he did, the light followed.

It tracked him alongside the road, for several miles, some distance out. Messinese sped up, and the light matched him.

Finally it seemed to move directly in front of him, and about a quarter mile ahead, visible even without his headlights, was a craft of some kind, something like an inverted saucer, flat on the bottom but something like a dome on the top. It shone brightly, light enough that stray farm buildings off the road showed up clearly. The officer described it as appearing to be about the size of a substantial house.

The object was still in the sky; Messinese had stopped, but it did not appear to block him from continuing. He focused on trying to cross an upcoming bridge, and was concerned that it might stop him from doing it.

That didn't happen. He continued on, across the bridge and toward I-15. The light moved back to the side, off in the distance. It followed him for a while, and then was gone. In all, from start to finish, Messinese figured he had spent forty-five minutes or more in the presence of . . . whatever it was.

The area has been full of UFO sightings over the years, most of them non-police-related. An example: The National UFO Reporting Center lists this report from Pocatello on June 24, 2002, from the early evening: "A very experienced pilot witnessed a strange-looking object pass below his aircraft at high speed. The object looked generally like the Space Shuttle, with no prominent wings, and appeared to the witness to be hugging the contour of the mountainous region below. It quickly disappeared from sight, within 15 seconds of the pilot's first sighting of it."

Idaho's history with UFOs, or at least reports of them, is extensive. What that means, and what weight you give to the various accounts, is up to you. Many interpretations are possible. In a June 16, 2009, column, Steve Crump, the longtime opinion editor at the Twin Falls *Times-News*, had this to say: "In Steven Spielberg's movie *Close Encounters of the Third Kind*, aliens abducted Richard Dreyfuss from Wyoming. But in Idaho in 1956, they took a steer. What does that say about us?"

CHAPTER 11

Haunted Penitentiary

"Haunted" is so often followed by "house" that we often forget more logical locations for hauntings.

Prisons, for example. Although, of course, a prison is sometimes referred to as a "big house."

The website American Hauntings lists the top ten haunted prisons, including some of the best known in the country: Alcatraz, the Eastern State Penitentiary in Pennsylvania, and the Wyoming Territorial Prison. Hauntings of some sort have been reported at many older jails and prisons around the country, and some newer ones.

The list makes sense: Many bad things (that in theory could inspire a haunting) can and do happen in prisons. People die there, sometimes in the course of bad acts—just the sort of things hauntings are supposed to be made of. Even the word "penitentiary" has spiritual roots, referring to the provision of penance for bad acts. Sometimes too executions are held at prisons, and a number of hauntings are said to be associated with those.

Several places associated with law enforcement in the Old West are reputed to have a haunting connection. Criminal activity and law enforcement pushback accounted for a significant number of deaths in the early days of Idaho City, located about forty miles up in the mountains northeast of Boise. Quite a few rough customers passed through the Boise County Jail and Pest House, as it was called. When they died, they were interred at either Boot Hill Cemetery or, if their reputation ranked a little higher, at the Pioneer Cemetery. Visitors to both of those places have reported, from time to time, seeing spectral beings and hearing unusual noises.

In his book *Haunted Old West*, writer Matthew P. Mayo reported of Idaho City that "some eyewitnesses of the Boot Hill specters say they don't feel frightened or threatened by them, but they do feel as if there is a great sense of sadness in the air, a palpable melancholia exuded by the wispy visions as they drift among and through the old tombstones and fences surrounding some of the gravesites."

Idaho City held its population and wild ways for only a few years. Within a decade many more people, and much more criminal activity and tragedy, congregated down the hill, miles downstream along the Boise River basin, in the new territorial capital—and the new territorial prison.

The old Idaho Penitentiary is the capital of haunted sites in Idaho. The group Big River Paranormal, a team investigating prospectively haunted locations in the Northwest, has sent its teams to the Idaho Penitentiary several times, including as recently as 2019—and rarely has come up empty. It has made far more trips to the old Idaho Pen than it has to any other location in the state.

This place is not the current, or new, penitentiary. Idaho has several relatively new correctional facilities scattered around the state, including on the southwest side of Boise, and none of those have alleged hauntings (at least as a recurring matter). The Old Pen, though, is a different story.

Walk up to and through it now—it's open for visits, and the state historical society offers tours and self-guided walks—and it has a somber, almost ancient feeling. The old sandstone buildings are decomposing, and many of them lack a roof. There's a sense of something like walking through Stonehenge when visiting the place.

And supposedly, there are lots of ghosts. The sober-minded Idaho Historical Society remarked on its website:

> While there is no conclusive evidence to suggest there are ghosts at this site, many visitors have seen and heard things they cannot explain. Some, including "Ghost Adventures," have captured strange/unexplainable images on their cameras, still others claim to hear voices or be physically touched. Most sense a "heaviness" or "strange feelings" when visiting the site, specifically in Siberia (solitary-confinement cells) and the Gallows Room in Maximum Security. We continue to leave it to the individual to decide for themselves whether this is a "haunted" site or not.

That is at least more open-minded—to the prospect of supernatural activity—than is typical for an official state government site. What is not in doubt is the extensive history, some of it strange in nature, in back of the place.

Idaho Territory was formed in 1863, about the same time its first large and stable settlements—around Boise and Idaho

City—were being built. Theoretical law enforcement came not far behind, and sheriffs and other peace officers quickly found a need for a place to house prisoners and suspects. The earliest makeshift facilities were considered beyond inadequate within a very few years. By 1870, money was found to build a single-block territorial prison, located a couple of miles northeast of Boise down what soon became one of Boise's showcase residential streets, Warm Springs Avenue. (The area was named for intensive geothermal activity that heated many of the homes in the area, but the prison never benefited from it.) The prison opened for business two years later.

Only portions of the old Idaho Penitentiary remain at the site in eastern Boise, though it is open for regular tours.
RANDY STAPILUS

The building was situated on the Boise River plain, a few hundred yards back from the river and just below steep foothills looming overhead. Thrift being a central consideration, the prison builders found the cheapest possible means to do the job: They used prisoner labor to construct the place, and hand-cut sandstone rock out of the nearby hills for building material. Hauling the sandstone blocks down the grade to the building site was hard labor indeed for many of those convicts. The quarry they used is uphill from the prison site, near what is now called Table Rock.

The light sandstone blockhouse was built to contain all the prisoners, all together in one group. There were no individual cells at first.

More buildings were soon added, these too made of sandstone carried down the hillside and cut into tight blocks. Prisoners were used to build nearly every structure on the campus. Three cell houses were built, eventually including individual cells. A dining hall, hospital, and barbershop were built, along with administrative offices and a house for the warden. Within a few decades, the prison held six hundred convicts at a time, and often was at full capacity or beyond it.

A wall was built to surround the whole complex and diminish chance of escape. It lessened them only somewhat; over the years there were five hundred escape attempts, and about a fifth of those were either temporarily or permanently successful.

The prisoners were well motivated to try to escape. The buildings were rough and basic. For decades after construction there was no heating system for the winter or cooling in the summer. The sandstone absorbed and retained the hot temperature, and seemed to cool beyond the ability to warm it in the cold. The first plumbing didn't enter the complex until around 1928, and even then, it was so primitive that disease often spread through the buildings. The nearly nonexistent ventilation didn't help. An estimated 110 prisoners died over the years because they succumbed to illness or old age or were murdered.

Many of Idaho's most famous criminals lived there for a time. Harry Orchard, who killed an Idaho governor along with more than a dozen other people, came to the prison in 1906 and stayed there until 1954, dying in the prison hospital. He admitted to assassinating Frank Steunenberg, the former governor of Idaho, and took responsibility for sixteen more killings besides; in addition to knocking around doing other sorts of odd jobs, he seems to have been a killer for hire. Although he confessed and thereby avoided a trial himself, he was a major figure in Idaho's one criminal trial of international renown, in which labor leader "Big Bill" Haywood and others were said to have put him up to the Steunenberg bombing. (They were acquitted.) Orchard actually found a calming and quiet life at the Old Pen, working in the shoe shop and chicken farm, and ended his life at the prison but outside prison walls, in a small cottage.

"Diamondfield" Jack Davis, a southern Idaho cattle hand and gunman for hire, spent months there until he was cleared of a double murder for which he nearly was hanged, after barely avoiding execution several times. He spent the last of his years behind bars at the penitentiary, leaving there when he received a gubernatorial pardon. He is widely believed to have been innocent of the killings, of a pair of sheepherders, for which he was convicted.

Lyda Southard, convicted of killing a string of husbands for their insurance money, was the best known of the women who served time there—and was also one of the most famous escapees. She was convicted of the poisoning death of her fourth husband, but her earlier three husbands, not to mention two other close relatives, all died in a similar way, and she has long been assumed to have killed them all. She originally was sentenced to a term of ten years to life in prison. When she was not released after ten years, she apparently decided she was taking off anyway and managed to escape. After fifteen months she was recaptured, and she spent more years in the prison before her release in 1941.

Southard was one of only a few female prisoners. The first of them were held in reconditioned office areas, in an administrative building, and in vacant spaces, such as unused storage rooms. In 1905, their numbers became just large enough to warrant a separate facility, which was created in the building formerly used by the warden as a residence, once male inmates built a large wall around it. A full women's ward was built in 1920.

Remarkably, for several generations the prisoners were—aside from escape attempts—mostly quiescent, well behaved. Small uprisings were reported in the 1930s, including a dining hall "near-riot" in 1935, but the first big riot came in May 1952. After a dispute involving the prison grievance committee, more than three hundred convicts rampaged for four hours through the facility, setting fire to the recreational hall and destroying windows and furniture. Their energy spent, they returned to their cells by evening. That led state officials to begin planning for building a new prison, this time in the desert south of Boise. But that work would take many years.

The next big riot came in August 1971 amid a heat wave, when fires wiped out two buildings and a couple of prisoners were stabbed. That helped accelerate work on the new prison, which got a soft launch later in the year.

In March 1973, an even more serious riot erupted at the Old Pen, when the chapel and a new dining hall were torched. The price tag for the damage this time was put at $100,000. By the end of that year, the last of the Old Pen prisoners were transferred out, and the old complex was decommissioned. It had been in operation for 101 years. The next year, it was listed on the National Register of Historic Places. The Idaho Historical Society operates the building and grounds today; it offers regular tours of the place.

The property in recent years has been carefully maintained, and the grounds include bright and attractive gardens. The old warden's house has been sharply maintained and is now used for state offices. The state arts commission also has been located on the grounds. But many of the Old Pen buildings now are a decayed version of what they once were. The central building, where the entrance and gift shop area are located, still evokes a feeling that must be similar to what the pen felt like shortly before its closure in 1973.

The only sort-of "active" part of the facility—still used for its original purpose—is the cemetery, located behind a gate by the nearby Idaho Botanical Gardens, a few hundred yards away.

Ten men were executed at the Old Penitentiary. The first, known simply as Tambiago, was hanged in 1878. There were no more until 1901—Edward Rice was the second—and a slow stream followed until 1926. For a quarter century no more were executed, but in April 1951 two were.

Many of the reports of spirits at the old prison are centered in specific rooms.
RANDY STAPILUS

Six of the executions were held in the Rose Garden, a place where a portable gallows could be readily set up. The Rose Garden is open to tourists, and some have reported seeing "apparitions" and feeling cold spots in the area.

The last person to be executed there, on October 16, 1957, was Raymond Allen Snowden, who was convicted of murdering one woman and confessed to killing two others; he has been referred to as Idaho's Jack the Ripper.

Snowden, originally from the New England region (details are sketchy), was a wandering laborer originally convicted of killing a woman from Garden City whom he had met at a nightclub— killing her by stabbing her twenty-nine times. He was caught and convicted quickly; his guilt was never seriously contested, and his execution followed his killing offense by only about a year.

Thirty-six-year-old Snowden was executed in the Gallows Room at the Number 5 House, which was used as a maximum-security facility. The site Hauntedrooms.com said, "It's believed that Snowden's spirit has never left the penitentiary. Many state that he has been haunting the grounds since his execution that fateful day in October of 1957."

His last reported words were, "I can't put into words what I want to say."

The Urban Legends Online site noted:

On the day of his hanging, the gallows was set up with a room with a glass window so the families of the victim could watch the hanging. When the officers pulled the lever the big iron trapdoors slammed against the side walls and broke the glass, Snowden's neck didn't snap so Snowden hung there for fifteen minutes struggling for air. The families sat there listening to Snowden gurgle and grunt. Now the Old Idaho Penitentiary is closed and is a museum, but there have been witnesses saying you can still hear Snowden still [sic] struggle for his last breath of air it [sic] can happen in the day or night but it won't happen unless you're alone in the bottom part of the gallows.

An MSN website listing ghost stories from around the country called him the "spookiest ghost in Idaho." Snowden was buried in an unmarked grave on the prison grounds.

Elsewhere in that building, another inmate of death row was reported to have cheated the executioner by leaping from the third floor to ground level and killing himself. Some people have reported seeing greenish lights around the location of his death, and some reported batteries dying around the same place.

Another site, haunted-places-to-go.com, reported:

One of the most common of all of the haunting tales of this prison occurs when individuals who visit the massive structure approach the chambers of the executioner. Many have entered this area, and have felt an immense feeling of sadness. These individuals have become quite anxious, and have felt a strong sense of dread. Many visitors have been so sensitive to the paranormal activity in this area of the prison that they have been overwhelmed emotionally, and cried, or they have become quite ill. Many who tour the facility have to end their tour at these chambers simply because they are so overcome with emotions and feelings of physical malaise.

More ghostlike images and "cold spots" have been reported in and around "Siberia," the solitary-confinement facility.

The regional research group Big River Paranormal has a Boise section, and it has devoted much effort to reviewing cases reported at the Old Pen. In the 2010s, it made repeated visits to the facility and seldom came away empty-handed. For 2019 the group planned nine investigative events scattered through the year, two of them events called "Sleepless in Stripes."

The following account, from July 27, 2018, is typical of their reports:

A guest reported being poked in the back outside 5 House prior to the investigation commencing. She felt a sudden cold spot in conjunction with being poked. In Siberia the team heard what sounded like a radio being turned on. It did not sound like music, but indistinct chatter taking place. They were not able to determine where the sounds were coming from. Outside Siberia they did not hear it, but inside they did. A cold spot was reported as following a particular guest all evening (name not given). In 4 House the team heard a lot of sounds like footsteps taking place. On second tier near cell 8, Casey heard what sounded like someone tapping on cell bars. The team received unexplained EMF [electromagnetic field] fluctuations on the MEL Meter devices. Casey heard a labored breath as they were entering 2 House.

About three weeks later another report noted this:

In 5 House Roberta heard footsteps and shuffling. In Death Row near Raymond Snowden's cell the team heard more shuffling and footsteps. In the Cooler Katie got feelings of unease, that she could not explain, but it felt "weird" according to her report of the situation. In Siberia a guest reported the sensation of a cold spot inside cell 10. In 4 House the MEL Meter died twice, especially after the battery having been changed out. On the second tier in 4 House, near cell 3 guests and the team smelled the odor of cigarette smoke. This was also smelled in front of cell 5. In 4 House beside cell 5, Katie L. heard what sounded like a male voice coming from behind her, this was also reported by a guest who claimed to have also heard this happen. While in the shirt factory (laundry room), the team reported seeing light anomalies coming from the shower area in conjunction with a whisper coming from or near the shower area.

The group's website noted this for prospective volunteers watching for spooky events:

Remember, ghosts, spirits, and the like do not perform on command. It is possible that we will have activity and it is possible that we may not. However, you never know for sure until all of the evidence from the night has been gone through. Many investigators will tell you that they did not think anything had occurred only to discover during the evidence review that an EVP [electronic voice phenomenon] with their name being whispered was captured at a location.

And the investigations go on.

CHAPTER 12

Shoshone Ice Caves

When you visit the Shoshone Ice Caves, you probably will arrive on a hot or at least warm day. The cave is closed from October through April, and during summer and the adjoining weeks things can get hot out here in the desert. The cave entrance is located on relatively flat desert land about midway between the small cities of Shoshone and Bellevue, and in summer the landscape for many miles around this area is parched and hot.

When you enter from the parking lot through the main visitor building, the large structure to the left (there's a small museum to the right), and walk past the gift shop to pay for a tour, you'll be pointed, even in the heat of summer when outside temperatures often hit triple digits, to a rack of large, warm, fluffy coats.

They aren't for sale, they aren't covered with logos, and they look out of place here. People who have traveled into working underground mines typically recall them as being hot and humid, not the kind of place where you'd think to add layers of clothing.

Still. You'd be strongly advised to pick one (there's no charge)—and you will be so advised by the local staff—because you'll need it for the tour. A few minutes after starting the tour, you'll be told, you'll be glad you had it. Most people seem to be skeptical at first, but most take the advice. Minutes later, they're glad they did.

Visitors on the guided tours are led through the back door of the visitors' building, which opens to a path laid with flat rocks, through massive lava craters, part of an immense formation that covers much of southern Idaho. The lava rock is still brittle and sharp, and stepping on it or even touching it is inadvisable; this area was hard to cross and hard to build upon.

You walk down a series of steep rock steps, about twelve hundred in all, and in a minute or so slip out of the sun, even at midday. You move into shade and then darkness alleviated only by human-made artificial lighting. Once, torches would have been needed to get so far.

From there, stepping down another dozen feet or so, you go from hot desert temperatures to a stunning freezer coldness—a drop of 60 degrees or more in the equivalent of walking from one floor to another in a building, only a dozen feet or so. Temperatures toward the bottom of the visitor area range from 23 to 33 degrees Fahrenheit year-round, with no artificial air-conditioning. Without that jacket you'd be shivering in a minute or so, and the ice cave tour has just begun.

A little lower and further underground, you're in a true winter cavern, a twilight zone of unusual sounds, optical illusions, geological formations sometimes called a "spangled fairyland," and ice floes where the temperature usually sits in the mid-20s.

It feels spookier than anyplace else in the state of Idaho. This is a place where the usual rules of simple reality seem to be suspended and the unexpected can happen. Little wonder that, in the decades and centuries before people began to understand how such a place came to be, it was regarded as a center of mystery and wonder.

Much of the northeastern portion of the desert of the Snake River Plain, the relatively flat part lying north of the Snake River in what is now southern Idaho, is covered by immense lava flows, and they started to get that way about sixteen million years ago, near what is now the three-state border between Idaho, Oregon, and Nevada.

Around that time and that place, a huge blob of molten material worked its way up from about fifty miles underground to much closer to the surface, melting rock and mineral as it went. The blob has not gone away or entirely cooled off. What has happened in the millions of years since it formed is the shifting of the earth's surface—the tectonic plate—above it. The "hot spot" (geologists call this the "hot spot theory") then moves on the surface, with changes something like a piece of paper moving while an ink pen writing below it stays still. The heated part of the surface has moved steadily east—on the surface—across what are now the Owyhee Mountains, into and through the northern Magic Valley, and farther east toward what is now Yellowstone National Park. That is where the hot spot resides today, as evidenced by geysers like Old Faithful and boiling pits along the landscape.

The results are more visible, even spectacular, in some places than others. Some are large enough to be easily observable from outer space. Some of the most spectacular are in what is now Craters of the Moon National Monument, a massive region drawing heavy tourist traffic, southeast of the Sun Valley area. The northern side of this area is called the Great Rift, which, according to the book *Roadside Geology of Idaho*, is a "world class geologic spectacular, a series of open fissures" running a vast distance across the desert.

Another large but less well-known area near Idaho Falls and Blackfoot, easily visible on I-15 between them, is Hells Half-Acre; part of it is designated as a national natural landmark. All of these areas are extremely rugged, and many of the lava flows look now much as they did hundreds of thousands or even millions of years ago. In some places, visitors are warned not to wear conventional shoes if they try to walk on the lava—the lava formations are still so sharp and rugged that ordinary soles would be sliced into pieces.

Then there is the big lava field to the west of Craters of the Moon, between the current cities of Shoshone and Bellevue, which looks less dramatic on the surface but in places is much more surprising in its developments underground. Large bubbles and heating vents developed throughout this area, allowing gases to escape from deep underground to the surface, in the process creating large and small caves unlike any found elsewhere in Idaho or, in a few cases, almost anywhere else at all. They can be hazardous to enter and explore, but they have been attracting people for thousands of years at least.

Several are popular visitor destinations, including the Mammoth Cave, a few miles north of Shoshone. It was formed, possibly hundreds of thousands of years ago, by a massive air bubble in the lava, and runs a quarter-mile long. The air bubble was all underground at first, but eventually some of the rock collapsed, and an opening to the surface appeared. It is thought to have been an ice cave in its earlier years, but no human has seen ice there. Animals found it; fossils of bears, buffalo, and early camels have been found there. Early human visitors to the region found it too, and a few of them seem to have lived there for a while.

More recent settlers found the cave opening in 1902 and explored it, but decided it was of little interest. Not until 1954 did a local high school student named Richard Olsen, in the process of hunting bobcats around the desert, rediscover it. He and his girl-friend Veneda brought a flashlight and walked through most of it, hoping to find buried treasure. He never did find any, but the cave captivated him. He obtained a title to the cave, under the Small Tract Act, and started raising mushrooms there.

The Mammoth Cave website reports:

In the sixties, during the Cold War, the government approached Richard and asked for the use of the cave for a civil defense shelter for people to come to get out of radiation if the United States was attacked. The Mountain Home Air Base was a target because of the big B52's loaded with hydrogen bombs that it always had ready to fly if we were attacked. They said they would gravel a good road to the cave if Richard would let them put food and supplies in the cave for 8000 people. They built a large platform and supplied food there for the next 20 years.

Shoshone Ice Caves, in what would be (but for some artifacts added by humans) an unremarkable spot on the desert floor a few miles north of that, is a different creature entirely. It too was formed by gaps and air bubbles in the lava, large tubes ranging from five to thirty feet in diameter, that were much larger than in the other locations. The size allowed a variety of geological events to develop over time.

As the geological "hot spot" moved east, the ground underneath the lava fields in the area cooled. The tubes allowed air to circulate in the underground area, and water—some of it natural moisture in the air—to enter as well. Probably the lava flows in the area also touched on the Snake River Aquifer, which runs in the area from almost a hundred miles to the northeast to almost a hundred miles to the southeast, and that too may have brought water into the underground system. The cool air, delivered through what amounted to a low-pressure wind tunnel, and the slight but steady underground water supply came together in the form of ice.

There are several ice caves in the region, mostly smaller than the Shoshone. The harder-to-reach Crystal Ice Cave, to the east, contains significant amounts of ice. The website for the Shoshone Ice Caves says, "The most unusual feature of the Ice Cave is that it is a natural refrigerator, creating a living glacier in an arid lava desert. The ice block is about 1,000 feet long and varies from 8 to 30 feet in depth." To this day, no one knows its exact or complete dimensions, because no one has plumbed its depths.

The cave was discovered and rediscovered over the millennia by Native American bands wandering over the area; the nearby neighborhood, dry and rocky, wasn't amenable to long-term settlement. They noticed the strange underground refrigerator, and legends about it developed over time.

One story is that a member of one of the bands (probably Shoshone), given the name Princess Edahow, mysteriously died at a young age. She was said to be buried in the cave, under the ice, waiting for the right time to reemerge. And the story goes that her spirit lives on there, haunting the cave. At least some visitors over the

The Shoshone Ice Caves are a rip in the south-central Idaho desert and made visible by man-made structures such as this statue of a Native American from the area.
RANDY STAPILUS

years have said things that give the impression there's some truth to that legend. The image of an ice princess seems to appear, from time to time, to visitors at the cave. Some natives took to calling it "the cave of mysteries."

Farmer settlers in the Gooding and Shoshone region came across the ice cave in the 1880s, and that is where its modern history begins. The northern side of what we now call the Magic Valley was a forbidding place then. It was a living hell for the earliest travelers from the east. Trekkers on the Oregon Trail had made their way through the Rocky Mountains, and one river basin and accompanying mountain range, only to hit—west of what is now Pocatello—a long stretch of flatland that felt as desolate as the Sahara. It was rocky desert; little beyond sagebrush and scrub grasses seemed to grow there. The wind roared at times, and the dust kicked up, with little vegetation to hold it down. There was little to eat, and—in the summer, when many of the travelers passed through the area—the unrelenting blaze of the sun could be deadly. The north side of the Snake River—still commonly known by locals as the "northside"—was the worst; most travelers veered south, even though the canyons and rivers encountered there could make the drive even more difficult. Native American tribes did not tend to stay long in this area.

The first settlers in the area near the ice caves, about a dozen miles to the south and east of it, were sheep and cattle owners who let their animals graze there intermittently. Real settlement here didn't begin until 1881, when the Oregon Short Line Railroad entered the area. (The first train would stop there two years later.) It was building a line running from Granger, Wyoming, northwest to Pocatello, then roughly west through to Nampa, across the Snake River Plain. It needed to set up a series of stops along the way, and one of those was marked at Shoshone, justified on the basis of the livestock trade in the area and the need to ship out large quantities of wool. That stop, and the later development of a crossroads of highways (U.S. Highways 26 and 93 and state highways 24 and 75) all merging together within a block of it, turned Shoshone into a small transportation hub. It was known as a rail town; the main street was called Rail Street.

In the 1880s, it became a lively, if still small, town, with a wide-ranging reputation as being "wide open." An early visitor named Carrie Strahorn reported of his stay there, "Ten and fifteen arrests per day were common and there was no other jail but a hole in the ground, with guards placed around the hole. There was a fight on the streets almost every hour of the day and night. Lot jumpers were numerous, bad whiskey was unlimited, dancehalls were on every corner, guns were fired at all hours and the loud time from gambling dens was ever vibrating through the air."

Shoshone was little more than a trailhead meeting place then, the T in the road where the newly developing Wood River Valley mining community to the north could meet with the east-west wagon trails that ran north of the Snake River. Farmers tentatively claimed land and took a crack at trying to raise crops in the area. It was on one of those trips around the region, no doubt, that a traveler spotted the ice cave and its unusual qualities.

When the railroad stop did develop at Shoshone, its residents quickly made their way north to the cave and began excavating ice from it—the only ice available, it was said, for a hundred miles around. The twenty-two bars then active in Shoshone—a notoriously tough town—had a region-wide reputation for especially cold beer.

The very idea of carting ice from a cave to town was a relatively new one, and would not even have been possible many decades before; practical iceboxes and storehouses did not even exist until the 1830s, and were not common until around the Civil War. But with their arrival at the Shoshone rail stop, residents could use saws, axes, and other tools to hack off large chunks of ice from the cave for their use. Natural ice in that era was becoming a valuable commodity in growing societies.

Shoshone would settle down and lose its tough-town reputation, but ice mining continued, providing ice for the people and
businesses of Shoshone until around the turn of the century. After
that, the quieter businesses of Shoshone needed less ice, and the
arrival of household refrigeration units early in the new century
dampened the need for ice from natural sources; now people could
make their own.

That wasn't the only use people found for the cave. Outlaws
attacking stagecoaches needed a place to escape and regroup, some-
place not too far off the trails between larger communities. Taking
a detour of a few miles across the lava fields—where following their
tracks would be especially difficult—and holing up in an obscure
air-conditioned underground cave sometimes proved an attractive
option in the late territorial days.

With more modern technology, the caves were visited less
often in the new century, but that is when its troubles began. Visitors in the 1920s and 1930s began tinkering with the structure of
the cave. In the 1930s, more development in the area ensued when
the Works Progress Administration designated the ice cave as a
work area, and a second entrance was hacked into the underground
structure. That was a problem, because the second set of air flows
quickly heated the cave, messing with the delicate flow of air. Most
of the ice in it then melted.

That created a crisis for the cave. For most of two decades
various people tried to find ways to reestablish the delicate balance
in air flow and temperature that kept the lower cave cold enough to
sustain and rebuild the ice. The answers were slow in coming.

The answers finally did emerge in 1954, with a man named Russell Robinson. Robinson had grown up not far away on the Snake River Plain, and he had long known about the cave, and knew it had been troubled for a couple of decades. He was an amateur geologist and became obsessed with restoring the cave to its natural state. Remarkably, over a period of many years, he succeeded.

An October 1994 article in the *Deseret News* of Salt Lake City said:

> Each year he would block up exposed openings and observe how it affected temperatures underground. Possessing extraordinary patience, he knew it would take years to see the most subtle changes. In the meantime, Robinson built a small curio shop and a 30-foot-high concrete Indian (a personal memorial to Chief Washakie of the Shoshones) to attract tourists off the main highway. He added a small museum and living quarters for his family, and by the 1970s his dream was becoming a reality. Slowly, the ice was returning.

Robinson was only forty-nine when he was killed in a traffic accident in 1981. For some years work on the ice cave halted, but eventually family members picked up the mantle. Dr. Henry Robinson operated the business for many years, until his death in December 2013. His son Charles Fred Cheslik took over at that point, with his wife Christine.

Today the Shoshone Ice Caves are a visible landmark on the otherwise wide-open highway between Shoshone to the south and Bellevue to the north. The exterior on the ground surface is unlike anything else in Idaho; it might remind some people of a tourist stop on old Route 66. You'll see a dinosaur crafted from concrete, a massive statue of an Indian—Chief Washakie—and a caveman. The main gift shop and museum inside has a selection of artifacts, souvenirs, and gems from around the region: turquoise, quartz, jasper, and petrified wood. Fossils are there to be viewed as well; it's an eclectic collection in geology.

The traffic along that road is substantial because the Wood River Valley—the Ketchum and Sun Valley area—lies directly north, and the largest population center in the region, Twin Falls, is due south. It's nonetheless easy to zip past on the straight, fast road. But if you do, you miss the giant dinosaurs, the Indians, and especially a set of caves unlike any other. An hour spent exploring a piece of the landscape that seems as if it should not be there would not be misspent.

CHAPTER 13

Was Butch the Robber?

Washington Street, also known as U.S. Highway 89 and also the main street of downtown Montpelier, runs straight by the old railroad tracks that once were the foundation of the community. In the middle of downtown, in between Aho's Espresso Deli on one side and something called the "Smallest Store in Montpelier" on the other, sits a tourist spot labeled the Butch Cassidy Bank Robbery Museum.

There's a large picture of Cassidy on a sign in front, and also a sign atop most of the others saying THE BANK OF MONTPELIER, EST. 1891. It is marked as a museum and a gift shop, and has been under renovation several times in recent years, as new exhibits have been added to the mix. The museum ordinarily is open most days from Memorial Day to Labor Day.

The spot actually is where the Bank of Montpelier was established and operated. Said to be the first state-chartered bank in the state of Idaho—possible, since Idaho was only a few months old as a state when the bank was founded—the place is a historic location in any event, though it has not been home to a bank in decades.

Montpelier has not been shy in recent years about promoting the bank robbery. It's an unusual tourist draw, but you use what you have. Montpelier carries it to the point of hosting an annual robbery reenactment and a bicycle chase (to be explained momentarily) off into the nearby hills, followed by a large barbecue dinner. All of it has helped give Montpelier, which in some ways has struggled economically, a bit of flair.

But there is an underlying question: Was it really Butch Cassidy who robbed the bank? The basic facts of the robbery—most of the facts, at least—are clear enough, including the fact that there was a bank and it was robbed.

The day was August 13, 1896; the bank was five years and four months old. The time was midafternoon, approaching three p.m. The day was hot, and in Montpelier it also was humid. The city is located just inland of the northern shore of Bear Lake (the land between the city and lake is marshland), and Bear Lake is one of the largest bodies of water in the region. People were not moving around rapidly, and for the most part kept to the shade in the well-treed city.

The horsemen who rode into town—from which direction was not certain, but probably from the southeast, toward Wyoming—were no doubt observed, but no special attention was paid. Montpelier was founded as a rail stop, so people passing through, or bringing a load in a wagon as happened on this afternoon, were not unusual to see.

Some people did remark later that they took note that the men were dressed better than the typical travelers of the day, almost urban in their relative finery. The horses' tack was new too, and of high quality. These men had some money, and that was unusual.

There were three horsemen, clopping steadily down Washington Street, leading a sorrel pack mare that was dragging behind.

They in turn observed the town as they passed, possibly noticing the differences between the two sides of Washington Street, which then formed a distinct demarcation between the Mormon and Gentile sections of town. The coming of the railroad there had led, and would lead for a few decades, to two distinct communities there.

At the 800 block of Washington Street they stopped and dismounted. Deliberately but with clear direction, they walked toward the building headed by the sign BANK OF MONTPELIER. One of them took the head of the horses and led them around the block to the back door of the building. The others walked to the front door.

Inside the building, conditions were cooler and darker; the afternoon sun was not yet low enough to beat through the windows. But most of the blinds were down to conserve the cool.

A few minutes before three p.m., the staff was preparing to close business—for public access—for the day. Their workday would continue for another two or three hours, but that was for bookkeeping and money management, work that had to happen only after the doors were closed and locked. The practice was standard then among banks, just as an operating principle; like almost all western banks at the time, the Bank of Montpelier was independent, not part of a chain. Customers were shooed out at three, if they could be persuaded; four of them were hanging around, talking casually. Cashier E. C. Gray was trying to manage that transition to shutting down, and his assistant, Bud McIntosh, was starting to collect the paperwork they would need for end-of-day recordkeeping. But Gray was a little frustrated, not only because the customers were standing around and talking, but because one of them, William Perkins, was a Montpelier City Council member and happy to talk at length with constituents and fellow bank customers. That was the scene when the newcomers quietly walked through the front door.

They were described later with some clarity. The apparent leader was a stocky man with blond hair and a large mustache; he seemed cool and relaxed, and had a friendly air about him. Another man was dark-haired, more jagged in his motion, tense, and gave the impression of being prone to violence. They did not cover their faces.

The impressions might have been influenced by what they did almost immediately once inside: They drew revolvers and kept them pointed in the general direction of most of the people in the room. The leader walked quickly to the side of the front door, keeping his back to the wall; his associate positioned himself in the middle of the room.

The leader's first words were remembered clearly: "Put your hands up, and keep your mouths shut. Face the closest wall. And keep your hands where I can see them." The bank employees and the customers followed those instructions.

The tall, dark-haired man stepped back to the counter where the tellers worked, and where McIntosh was now standing motionless. He produced an empty sack, put it down on the counter in front of McIntosh, and ordered it filled with however much money was available.

McIntosh paused, and his eyes may have flickered with a degree of indecision. The reason was that the bank had prepared for this eventuality: Below the counter they had placed a Winchester rifle. Should he try to reach it? He might be killed, or even if not, a bloodbath might ensue.

The tall robber may have sensed something—in the indecision at least—and swung his revolver around at McIntosh, smacking him in the forehead, sending him sprawling away from the counter. McIntosh froze once more, and the robber seemed about ready to come over the counter and attack him.

The leader yelled over at him, "Just get the money!"

Apparently ignoring the Winchester—the accounts are a little vague on what happened to it—the tall robber moved behind the counter and rapidly grabbed all the cash, coin, gold, and other valuables. But the leader evidently had been referring to another bag of money as well, a small bag placed on the counter by the bank as a promotional gimmick: a bag of gold coins, intended to prove (in those days before banking regulation or federal insurance) that the bank in fact was solvent. He grabbed that too.

How much it all amounted to, in actual value, was never clearly established. At least one of the robbers later would estimate the takings at about $7,000. Estimates from other quarters (including the bank's) ranged upward to $16,500.

They did not get everything in the bank. There were locked drawers, and a locked vault, not yet breached. The tall man was starting to bark orders aimed at those when the lead robber called out another instruction: "That's enough. We're done here."

Now the leader moved to the center of the room and waved at the bank employees and customers casually with his revolver. He told them to bunch together toward the back of the bank and stay there. He told them not to move and to stay quiet for ten minutes; as long as they did that, no harm would come to them. The men in the group signaled their agreement. With that, the robbers fled out the back door.

Gray, McIntosh, and the four customers reacted cautiously. They thought they heard four horses departing, but couldn't be completely sure. They seemed to be leaving the bank almost as casually as they had approached; they were not racing away, or did not seem to be.

The former hostages waited a few minutes—probably not the full ten—and tried to figure out what to do next. They were infuriated and humiliated, and wanted the robbers caught.

Gray cautiously opened the back door and saw no sign remaining of the robbers. He dashed back through the bank and out the front door, in search of law enforcement. But this was not so simple an operation as it might be today. Montpelier did not yet have a police department, so where he ran was to the telegraph office, to send an emergency telegram to the Bear Lake County sheriff, Jeff Davis. Davis, and his office, were located about a dozen miles away at the county seat in the town of Paris.

Davis happened to be immediately available, was on the case straightaway, and by about four p.m. was in Montpelier collecting facts and a sheriff's posse to chase after the robbers. Word from witnesses in town was that horsemen had headed east, out along the Montpelier Canyon Road, in the direction of the Wyoming line—probably the direction from which they had come.

The posse got a fast start. One story was that they employed a newfangled mode of transportation—a bicycle—to help alongside

The Butch Cassidy Museum now is a centerpiece of tourism activities in downtown Montpelier.

JAKE PUTNAM

the horses in giving chase. Odds are the bicycle didn't make good time over the very rough canyon roads.

The posse did head out for miles through the mountains, but dark fell before they got very far. Nor did they make much progress in the days afterward. Instead, Davis sent word ahead to Wyoming, hoping for help from law enforcement there.

He did have a theory about the case, which influenced how he conducted his search. Davis had an almost immediate suspect: Tom McCarty. McCarty was a known figure in the Montpelier area, mostly because he had courted and married his wife in the town. Davis also knew McCarty as a longtime suspect in a string of regional bank robberies (not any near Montpelier, though), and the style of this robbery sounded a lot like his. McCarty was known to spend much of his time in Wyoming's Star Valley, just east of the Idaho border not far from Montpelier. Davis contacted law enforcement there and waited to hear back.

Before long, he assembled another posse and rode with them to Star Valley. He did find a sorrel mare that looked much like the one the gang was said to have used, but that was thin evidence.

Over time, Davis collected more information: the descriptions of the robbers—whose faces were clearly seen—and the McCarty gang, who were known around the region. What he found was that the descriptions did not match, did not even come close. He finally concluded that he was chasing the wrong people.

Descriptions of the robbers were sent around the region. In September, on the far side of Wyoming, in Cheyenne, a railroad detective spotted an itinerant who he thought might have been involved in a railroad robbery. The man he arrested, Bob Meeks, was soon cleared of that incident, but partly because he offered up an alibi—one that put him in southeastern Idaho at the time of the Montpelier robbery. His description of his activities matched with local residents' clear description of the man who had held the horses at the back door of the bank while the robbery was taking place. He was extradited to Idaho and charged with robbery.

The Bear Lake County prosecutor was Alfred Budge, who later would go on to serve for decades on the Idaho Supreme Court and became especially notable regionally for this case. Although the witnesses were less than totally conclusive—Gray was a key witness, though he admitted he had never seen Meeks inside the bank—the conviction was a slam dunk. More than a year after the robbery, Meeks was transported to the Idaho State Penitentiary in Boise, where he became one of the more famous inmates. He tried to escape twice, losing a leg in the second attempt, but was released in 1912. He headed east, working on ranches, and spent most of the rest of his life in Colorado.

Although Meeks was the only robber convicted of the Montpelier heist, his trial made a splash because he offered details of what happened and who was involved. He said that the pack mare had carried the money into the hills independently of the three robbers, which offered some relative security for the money—in case one or more of them was caught—but also meant they had to double back and wander in the hills searching for her, or split up and go their separate ways, until they found her. That random pattern may have led them away from the posse.

The tall, dark-haired man, Meeks said, was Elzy Lay, a frequent outlaw who had worked with several gangs. Never brought in for the Idaho robbery, he was captured by law enforcement later for another one in New Mexico. After his release from prison for that, he went into the oil business and made money in that arena until his death in 1933.

The third man, Meeks said, the coolheaded leader of the bunch, was Robert Leroy Parker—his legal name—better known even then around the West as Butch Cassidy. He too was never charged or arrested for the Montpelier robbery. Meeks's testimony, the word of a veteran bank robber, is by far the strongest single piece of evidence that Cassidy was the leader of the gang.

It was enough that law enforcement circulated posters with Cassidy's picture, associating him with the robbery and offering a

$4,000 reward for his capture, "dead or alive." No one ever collected the reward money.

So, was Meeks telling the truth? Was Montpelier a Butch Cassidy heist? Probably. Not definitely.

The Montpelier robbery did fit, roughly, into Cassidy's life story. Or rather, Parker's.

Robert Leroy Parker—his legal name throughout his life—was born in Beaver, Utah, into a large rural Mormon family. His parents ran into financial trouble, and they all moved to another small community called Circleville, where Parker mostly grew up. The early financial issues, which involved either a bank or wealthier people in the area as the family's antagonists, led Parker to see himself eventually as a Robin Hood of sorts, and his periodic gifts in the backcountry to farmers and other people helped ensure his getaways from criminal activities and kept his hideouts well hidden. But he was motivated in other ways too. One quote attributed to him said, "The best way to hurt them is through their pocket book. They will Holler louder than if you cut off both legs. I steal their money just to hear them holler."

He trained for a while as an assistant to a butcher—the origin of his long-time "Butch" nickname—and worked with, or for, a rancher (or ranch hand—the accounts vary) named Cassidy, whose name he adopted. He became involved in horse trading and transport, and was thought to be involved in rustling and possibly some small-scale stealing. His friends also included some more violent criminals, but when in 1894 he was arrested in Wyoming, the charge was for buying (for $5) a single horse that had been stolen.

For that offense he was sentenced to be locked up in the Wyoming penitentiary in Laramie for two years.

He got out early, after eighteen months, though there are conflicting stories as to how that happened. The more likely story is that the prosecutor's case had been flawed, with bad instructions given to the jury; the state had failed to prove that Cassidy (or Parker) had known the horse he bought was stolen. The better story is that Cassidy made a promise to Wyoming state officials that he would confine his criminal activities to locations outside the state of Wyoming. If the second story is true, the state didn't get satisfaction, though several years would pass before he engaged in robberies there.

Cassidy apparently was active as a robber before his sentence, even if he wasn't charged with or convicted of that crime. The first robbery he is generally thought to have been associated with was of the San Miguel Valley Bank in Telluride, Colorado, which seems to have been led by the McCarty brothers—the same crew Bear Lake County Sheriff Davis originally thought was the culprit of the robbery there. There's not much proof Cassidy was involved there, however; newspapers at the time did note other robbers, including the McCartys, but not Cassidy. Before his imprisonment, Cassidy seems to have spent much of his time working on ranches and trying to develop one of his own near Dubois, Wyoming.

After his release, which came in the spring of 1896, he seems to have decided that robberies would constitute his new career path. He gathered a collection of friends and fellow outlaws and found a useful hideout in a remote Wyoming hillside called the Hole in the Wall, named for an unusual cave structure. The group, variously known as the Cassidy Gang or the Hole-in-the-Wall Gang or the Wild Bunch (named for an earlier group of western outlaws), became the most famous robbery outfit of the day.

Its members included Dick Maxwell, Bob Meeks, and William "Elzy" Lay; later additions would include the most famous, Harry Longabaugh, better known as the "Sundance Kid," though most evidence suggests that he had not yet joined the group as of 1896.

The Cassidy gang would be credited with many robberies across several western states and territories over the next eight years. The first of them was the robbery in Montpelier, executed only about five months after Cassidy's release from prison. That would allow just about enough time to set up the gang, establish the hiding place, and properly case the target (a routine Cassidy carefully practiced for years). One reason law enforcement in Bear Lake did not immediately think of them was that they hadn't been very active in the field until then (as opposed to the McCartys, who were).

The capture and conviction, and apparent guilt, of Bob Meeks, an active member of the gang at that time, is the main connecting link between Montpelier and Butch Cassidy. If Cassidy did lead that heist, it marked an important point in his career: his first major robbery in a long string of them as the leader of the criminal group. And a successful robbery at that.

The odds favor that view. Proving it is another matter.

The outlines of what is broadly presumed to have happened to Cassidy are loosely covered in the 1969 movie *Butch Cassidy and the Sundance Kid*. He became too successful and was pursued across the West. He and Longabaugh finally fled the country, arriving in South America. The most common account of what happened to him is that he was shot to death in Bolivia in 1908, though hard evidence of that is sketchy. Some contrary narratives have him returning to the United States after several years and living quietly until his death in Spokane, Washington, in 1937. Again, proof is hard to come by.

The fate of the Bank of Montpelier is clearer. It easily survived the great robbery of 1896, but folded during the bank crashes of the early Great Depression. Too many customers actually had decided, at that point, that their money wasn't safe there. But Butch Cassidy had nothing to do with that.

CHAPTER 14

The Iron Door

Somehow, it's not always enough to have a plain old buried treasure. Sure, there may be plenty of fictional cases, from *Treasure Island* on through the years, and even some real ones, but something more really seems to be needed to give the story some extra sizzle. In the American West, in a surprising number of cases, that something extra has turned out to be an iron door.

Iron doors have popped up repeatedly in American buried-treasure stories. One of the best-selling American writers of the first half of the twentieth century, Harold Bell Wright, wrote about one of them in a book called *The Mine with the Iron Door* (published by D. Appleton and Company in 1923). He wrote a wide range of articles and stories, ranging from nonfiction to inspirational Christian stories (he was also a minister in several communities) to science fiction. Where among these various types of writings he classified *The Mine with the Iron Door* isn't clear. He lived at the time in southern Arizona, and the mine was said to be located some miles north of Tucson, in the Santa Catalina Mountains.

He was in any event retelling a regional story that spread through newspapers in the American Southwest for half a century, beginning in the 1880s and 1890s, about various people who claimed to have found a lost city—or, failing that, a mine with associated treasures within—behind a massive iron door.

The tales speak of a Father Silvestre Velez de Escalante, who traveled with the well-known (and historically established) Father Eusebio Kino, who planted Jesuit missions around the Southwest in the years around 1700. Escalante was said to have found a rich deposit of gold somewhere in the mountains, and enslaved natives living nearby to extract it. The area was called Canada del Oro, or Gold Gulch. The gold was said to have gone to various places: some back to Spain, some to people around the region, and some left in place. The Jesuits were driven out of the region in 1767, and the story says they left much of the rich findings in place behind an iron door to keep out their adversaries.

Almost certainly there was a kernel of truth here. A 1994 report by the United States government reviewing mining activity in the West said: "Gold placering in Canada del Oro ('gold gulch') was undertaken in the northern Santa Catalina Mountains by Spaniards as early as the mid-1700's." The stories are conflicting and confused; some stories refer to active gold mining in the area in the late 1700s, after the Jesuits had left, and another man also named Escalante shows up in some stories. There are also iron door mining stories from the area that have nothing to do with Escalante.

Arizona had a gold rush of its own in the 1880s, and as people poured in and new newspapers sought circulation, the tales of the Escalante mine gained renewed attention. No one, however, ever found either the mine or the door, though some mining did happen in the Santa Catalina Mountains.

There were other iron door stories around the West too.

California has a couple of old, abandoned mines that were called—despite lacking the distinctive namesake barrier—iron door mines, the origin of the names in those cases being exceedingly obscure. Oregon and New Mexico also have tales of semilegendary iron door treasures in remote places.

Western historian Robert Zucker has written of another iron door report near Lawton, Oklahoma, with an especially colorful story attached:

> The Lost Cave With the Iron Door in the Wichita Mountains near Lawton, Oklahoma reportedly contained $11 million in Spanish gold ingots and doubloons. A heavy iron door closed off the entrance. The skeletons of 17 Indians guarded the treasure. A strange twist to the story involves outlaw Jesse James. He was reported to have stored two thousand dollars of loot in the cave. Other stories suggest that Belle Starr also stored $500,000 in the cave. The rumors drove so many prospectors to those mineral hills in 1897 that soldiers from nearby Fort Sill had to eject them.

None of these stories can quite match the persistence of, or the local response to, the story of the iron door in the Samaria Mountains near Malad, Idaho, even though no one knows for sure whether there's a real, actual treasure involved. And that story became an established part of local lore well before the Arizona tales gained currency in the Southwest.

Native Americans, fur trappers, military units, and others passed through the Malad Valley of Idaho for years before anyone gave serious thought to settling there. It was parched desert land and did not seem a likely spot to settle down and prosper. For a long time the area had a bad reputation; the nearby Malad River, for which the town was named, was said to have gotten its name as a place where a group of trappers had gotten a bad case of food poisoning. *Malad* is French for "sick," and the word translates to the English "malady." When people did appear in the valley regularly in numbers, they showed up for two starkly different reasons. One of those reasons was purely for transportation.

About a year after gold was found in northern Idaho at Pierce in 1862, prospectors located another large supply of the yellow metal to the east, in what is now Montana. Gold was spotted in an array of locations, given colorful names such as New Jerusalem, Marysville, Bon Accord, and Dogtown, but centered around a town called Bannack. (The word is derived from the name of an Indian group, more commonly rendered as Bannock and now used as the name of the county for which Pocatello, Idaho, is the seat.) Founded in 1862, Bannack was a typical boomtown, growing to ten thousand people in a matter of months and, for a few seasons, producing a lot of gold.

But where could they send this gold; to whom could they sell it? No easy way, not even any good trails, existed to head west over the Bitterroot Mountains—and the Continental Divide that ran along it. A few people tried to conduct commerce along what has since become known as the Magruder Corridor, but as chapter 9 points out, the early history of human commerce there was difficult and unfortunate. After the Magruder killings, little serious attempt was made to expand the trade routes from Montana west.

The iron door is said to be located somewhere in these Samaria Hills, but has eluded rediscovery.
RANDY STAPILUS

The best answer, Montana locals concluded, was to create a long road headed south, to the only inland community then in existence that could commercially manage the gold: Salt Lake City. There were mountains, but available passes were low and could be managed through much of the year, much more easily than over the Bitterroots. A route was developed that ran roughly along the track of the present-day I-15, running from Montana through eastern Idaho—through what are now Idaho Falls and Pocatello, and south through the Malad Valley—south to Utah.

It was a rugged trail and carried its risks, mainly from other people. Those who used it in the 1860s and early 1870s were open to attack, either by native tribes or by robbers. Sometimes the lines between the trustworthy and the unscrupulous were hard to observe; one of the early sheriffs in Bannack was Henry Plummer, known to moonlight as a notorious outlaw. Such attacks were not unknown, all the way along the route. One of the most spectacular robberies along it, more than one hundred fifty miles north of Malad (and led by an Idaho sheriff from Boise), is recounted in chapter 4.

The route got heavier use around the time, in 1869, when the golden spike united the two sides of the first transcontinental railroad in Utah, and traffic between Montana and the outside world increased at about the same time gold mining in the area began to diminish.

As the road was developed heading south, so were people from the Salt Lake Valley looking north. The Malad Valley was among the regions in southeastern Idaho spotted as prospective expansion territory by leaders of the Church of Jesus Christ of Latter-Day Saints in Salt Lake City, and church president Brigham Young was among those who came north to explore the area. The timing happened to mesh closely with the development of the stage lines from Montana south to Utah, and for purposes of creating credible tales of missing gold, that may be significant.

The small town of Malad developed in the valley first, but some settlers (most though not all of them coming from Utah) spread out around the valley. The first to arrive in the tracts to the west of that town was a Utah settler named John Evans Price, who recalled in his diary, "On February 10, 1868, I took up 160 acres of land eight miles west of Malad. I went with my sons and built a dugout on the claim. I sold my place in Malad for a wagon and yoke of oxen. On April 16, 1868, I moved my family here, and we were the only white residents. The country was covered with sagebrush and inhabited only by the American Indians and the wild beasts."

That area, about eight to ten miles west of Malad but still in the valley, was near a settlement called Samaria, after the town mentioned in the Bible. It was lightly hemmed in by the hills around it, especially toward the south and west, which were called the Samaria Hills, and those in turn were foothills of mountains that extended for many square miles off into the distance. Samaria became the largest community in the valley for a time, until railroad service chose to use the more direct route and connect to Malad, a few miles to the east, instead. Samaria, along with its neighbor community, Gwenford, was cut out of the commercial mainstream and remained a small community of farmers and ranchers, just a few miles off the main trail—including the old Gold Road trail—that passed through Malad. The mountains beyond it were easily accessible but lightly traveled, not a bad place to go for someone who wanted to keep out of sight. Or to keep their belongings from prying eyes.

Around Malad and Samaria, communities well accustomed to travelers passing through, a story long circulated about a lone rider on horseback who rode through the valley and finally sought attention from a local homestead. The story, as told on a Malad city historical website, said:

[As the man] came closer they sensed that something was wrong. The horse moved at a slow pace, and the rider nearly collapsed in the saddle. Soon they could see that he was wounded. They hurried to the horse, helped him down, and carried the almost unconscious man to their cabin. He had been shot at least twice, and had lost a lot of blood.

As they laid him on the bed he began to talk. The story he told was this:

He was an outlaw and for several years had robbed the stage lines which sent their coaches through the valley. He had thrown in with two others, and the three of them had accumulated a great deal of stolen gold. They hid their stolen wares in a cave in the mountains south of the town called Samaria. They had sealed the entrance to the cave with an iron door. As he explained his story the homesteaders learned that he had been shot by the other robbers during an argument. However, he had killed the other two and placed their bodies in the cave with the gold and sealed it with the iron door. He had been too weak to take the gold with him. As he continued to worsen he offered a poor description of the cave's location, only saying that it was near the top of one of the peaks where the view offered escape from any approaching posse.

That story doesn't have an ending: There's no explanation for what became of the mysterious traveler.

But the more immediate story, the one that has kept the subject alive in local minds in the century and more since, picks up in 1891. It centers on Glispie Waldron, who was born in 1878 in Samaria. His family, which had made one of the original pioneer claims in the area and set up a ranch in nearby Gwenford, tended crops and cattle in the high mountain fields there. As a boy, Glispie Waldron's job was to help with all of that, including watching over the family's collection of working horses.

One day in 1891, probably in the fall, young Waldron was walking up in the Samaria Hills tracking down several horses that had wandered away. The old history of the Malad Valley, written early in the twentieth century and carefully maintained at the Oneida County Pioneer Museum in Malad, describes what happened:

One day while Glispie was on his horse gathering the family's horses in the mountains, he came upon an iron door that seemed to cover the opening of a mine. He had to keep up with the horses, so he hung his jacket where he could come back and find it so he could investigate the door and mine more carefully.

Unfortunately when he returned, he was unable to find his jacket or the iron door. He was about 12 years old at the time.

Over the years the iron door became quite a legend with many stories being written about it and what might be behind it.

How he determined that the door was made of iron, rather than of some other metal, is unclear. And there was no especially detailed description of the door, or how it was secured. It soon became part of the local legend and lore, but it was not dismissed as a fantasy.

For one thing, Waldron was not a fly-by-night person prone to fanciful storytelling. He lived in the Samaria area his whole life until his death in 1962, farming, marrying, and raising fourteen children. He was described—and is described even today—as honest, stable, clearheaded, and reputable. The Waldron family was well established there too; as some of the first settlers in the area, they founded much of Samaria's early commerce. Connections remain between the early settlement and Samaria today; many of the people who live in the area now are descended from the first settlers there.

Waldron said the door looked as if it was made from two wagon wheels and an iron sheet, and his description of the location roughly matched that given by the wayward robber.

The local Malad history also noted:

A local man who was well acquainted with Glispy has spent a considerable time over the years searching for the Iron Door using Glispie's description. This same man has found evidence that coincides with the legend. Digging with hand tools and blasting with dynamite, he uncovered an assortment of bones and bone fragments that were later sent to a nearby university for analysis. The bones were found to be human remains.

People in the area, and fortune seekers from far away as well, have been checking it out ever since. From time to time, they still do.

In the late 1950s, a Malad kid named J. D. Williams, a member of a large family in the area, moved with his family from a house in town to the family's ranch in the Samaria-Gwenford area. In his teens at the time, he was responsible among other things for making sure the family's cattle were properly grazed. That was done in an area near the ranch, in the hills to the south and east of the community, on land operated by the Samaria Grazing Association.

Williams met the neighbors, including the Waldrons, and including Glispie Waldron; they were well established and highly regarded by their neighbors, he would recall. He never talked with Glispie directly about the iron door, but he heard the stories, as everyone in the area had, and like other neighbors worked out in rough terms where the decades-old sighting would have been.

Moving cattle through the grazing area, he sometimes would ride his horse along the back side of the Samaria Hills toward an area called Portage, and then along a rough road close by the Idaho-Utah state line. Then, in line with where the cattle grazed, he would veer north again, back into Idaho, and look up into the folds of the mountains. Somewhere in there it must be, he thought.

He rode back up into those hills several times, working the cattle and also keeping his eyes open for what he had heard might be back there. He was not alone; plenty of other people from the area, including others who also ran their cattle through the region, did the same, in years before and in years since. They looked carefully, but none of them ever quite found what they were looking for.

Williams would go on to find his personal future in other places. In the years to come he became an attorney, later mayor of the nearby city of Preston, Idaho state auditor and controller, a candidate for high office, and an executive in several large high-tech corporations. From time to time he would revisit the family holdings in Samaria, walk around them, and think about the history and people and legends of the place.

And look up into the Samaria Hills. And wonder.

BIBLIOGRAPHY

Alt, David D., and Donald W. Hyndman. *Roadside Geology of Idaho*. Missoula, Mont.: Mountain Press Publishing Company, 1989.

Anderson, Tim. *Smokey and the UFO: UFO Encounters by Idaho State Police*. Seattle: Amazon Digital Services, 2017.

Bear Lake Rendezvous Chamber of Commerce. "Bear Lake Monster." Accessed June 5, 2019. https://web.archive.org/web/20130809175009/http://bearlakechamber.com/bearlakemonster.aspx.

Bear Lake Valley Convention & Visitors Bureau. "Butch Cassidy History." Accessed June 8, 2019. https://bearlake.org/butch-cassidy/.

Bigfoot Field Researchers Organization. www.bfro.net.

Big River Paranormal. "Old Idaho Pen." Accessed October 9, 2019. www.bigriverparanormal.com/old-idaho-pen.html.

Blewer, Mac. "Butch Cassidy in Wyoming." WyoHistory.org. November 8, 2014, accessed June 8, 2019. www.wyohistory.org/encyclopedia/butch-cassidy-wyoming.

Boudreaux, Crandal. "Shoshone Ice Cave—All That's Missing Is the Beer." *Boise the Great*. Accessed June 9, 2019. www.boisethegreat.com/articles/shoshoneicecave.php.

Bunderson, Hal, ed. *Idaho's 200 Cities, the East*. Carlton, Oreg.: Ridenbaugh Press, 2018.

———. *Idaho's 200 Cities, the North*. Carlton, Oreg.: Ridenbaugh Press, 2018.

———. *Idaho's 200 Cities, the Southwest*. Carlton, Oreg.: Ridenbaugh Press, 2018.

Carlson, Chris. *Mediment Reflections: 40 Years of Issues and Idahoans*. Carlton, Oreg.: Ridenbaugh Press, 2013.

Carrington, A., ed. *The Latter-day Saints' Millennial Star*, Vol. 30, 1868.

Conley, Cort. *Idaho for the Curious: A Guide*. Cambridge, Idaho: Backeddy Books, 1982.

———. *Idaho Loners: Hermits, Solitaries and Individualists*. Cambridge, Idaho: Backeddy Books, 1994.

Courtwright, David T. *Dark Paradise: A History of Opiate Addiction in America*. Cambridge, Mass.: Harvard University Press, Enlarged edition, 2001.

Edwards, William. "Copper Camp Mining Company Inc.—A Prospectus." Edwardsburg, Idaho: date unlisted.

Frasure, Chelsea. "Urban Legends: The Native American Water Babies." HubPages. September 19, 2016, accessed June 8, 2019. https://hubpages .com/education/Urban-Legends-The-Native-American-Water-Babies.

Graff, Henry F. *Grover Cleveland*. New York: Times Books, 2002.

Guiley, Rosemary Ellen. *Atlas of the Mysterious in North America*. New York: Facts on File Books, 1995.

Halfmoon, Otis. "Lewis and Clark through Nez Perce Eyes." Discovering Lewis & Clark. Accessed June 9, 2019. www.lewis-clark.org/article/984.

Hamilton, Ladd. *This Bloody Deed: The Magruder Incident*. Pullman: Washington State University Press, 1994.

Hart, Arthur A. *Basin of Gold: Life in Boise Basin, 1862–1890*. Boise, Idaho: Historic Boise, Inc., 1990.

———. *Chinatown: Boise, Idaho, 1870–1970*. Caldwell, Idaho: Caxton Press, 2002.

Hesley, Marianne. "Legend and History of Spirit Lake, Idaho." Spirit Lake, ID. Accessed June 8, 2019. www.spiritlakeid.gov/history/.

HistoryNet.com. "Butch Cassidy." Accessed June 9, 2019. www.historynet .com/butch-cassidy.

Holbrook, R. L. "Lewiston Water Treatment System Designed to Prevent Teeth Decay; Science Will Study Future Result." *Lewiston Tribune*, July 5, 1947.

Hughes, Clarence Ralph, ed. *We the People of Samaria*. Malad, Idaho: Exemplar Press, 2010 (2nd ed.).

Idaho Sheriff's Association. "History of Idaho Sheriff's Offices." 1998.

Idaho Supreme Court. *Digest of the Decisions of the Supreme Court of Idaho: Covering All Cases Reported in Volumes 1 to 24, Idaho Reports*, n.d.

Idaho's Mammoth Cave. "The Biggest Show under the Earth." Accessed June 8, 2019. www.idahosmammothcave.com.

Internet Archive. "Full Text of 'National UFO Reporting Center recordings, 1974 to 1989.'" Accessed June 8, 2019. https://archive.org/stream/ NationalUfoReportingCenterRecordings1974To1989/NuforcDirectory _djvu.txt.

Jameson, W. C. *Butch Cassidy: Beyond the Grave*. Lanham, Md.: Taylor Trade Publications, 2012.

Jandals and Jet Planes. "Robbing Banks in the Wild Wild West." Accessed June 8, 2019. https://jandalsandjetplanes.wordpress.com/2018/09/05/robbing -banks-in-the-wild-wild-west/?fbclid=IwAR1-7S1qX3or4xxzkF-OF1gQX cbC0AlXW1x2QB8gxkDXo92LHS9FYmfzo.

Jensen, Dwight William. *Visiting Boise: A Personal Guide*. Caldwell, Idaho: Caxton Printers, 1981.

Josephy, Alvin M. *The Nez Perce Indians and the Opening of the Northwest*. Boston: Houghton Mifflin, 1965.

Just, Rick. *Idaho State Parks (Images of America)*. Mount Pleasant, S.C.: Arcadia Press, 2017.

Kootenai Tribe. http://kootenai.org/history.html.

Langford, Nathaniel. *Vigilante Days and Ways*. Helena, Mont.: Farcountry Press, 1995.

Legends of America. "Butch Cassidy & the Wild Bunch." Accessed June 8, 2019. www.legendsofamerica.com/butch-cassidy/.

Legends of America. "More Idaho Treasure Tales." Accessed June 9, 2019. www .legendsofamerica.com/more-idaho-treasure/.

Loeffler, Fred. *The Avenging Innkeeper: Magruder Party Murder*. Melba, Idaho: Yates Publishing, 1972.

Lukas, J. Anthony. *Big Trouble: A Murder in a Small Western Town Sets Off a Struggle for the Soul of America*. New York: Simon & Schuster, 1997.

Lustiger, Alan. "The 'State' of Idaho: The Case for Open Debate." Fantasymaps .com. Accessed October 9, 2019. www.fantasymaps.com/stuff/idaho.html.

Lyon, Suzanne. *Bandit Invincible: Butch Cassidy, a Western Story*. New York: Five Star, 2000.

Magnuson, Richard G. *Coeur d'Alene Diary: The First 10 Years of Hardrock Mining in North Idaho*. Portland, Oreg.: Metropolitan Press, 1968.

Mayo, Matthew P. *Haunted Old West: Phantom Cowboys, Spirit-filled Saloons, Mystical Mine Camps and Spectral Indians*. Guilford, Conn.: Globe Pequot Press, 2012.

McDevitt, Tom. *Ligertown*. Pasadena, Calif.: Little Red Hen, 2002.

McNeel, Jack. "New Book Says Lewis and Clark Couldn't Have Survived without Nez Perce." Indian Country Today. October 5, 2013, accessed June 9, 2019. https://newsmaven.io/indiancountrytoday/archive/new -book-says-lewis-and-clark-couldn-t-have-survived-without-nez-perce -tgmrl5El3EmGy8ZMdHJjCA/.

Moon, J, Howard, and Russell M. Tremayne. *A History of the Twin Falls Canal Company, 1905–2005*. Twin Falls, Idaho: Twin Falls Canal Company, 2005.

Ohlheiser, Abby. "'Basically, They Just Fell out of the Sky.' 2,000 Snow Geese Found Dead in Idaho." *Washington Post*, March 17, 2015, accessed June 3, 2019. www.washingtonpost.com/news/speaking-of-science/ wp/2015/03/17/basically-they-just-fell-out-of-the-sky-2000-snow-geese -found-dead-in-idaho/?noredirect=on&utm_term=.70c13ce85e52.

Patterson, Richard. *Butch Cassidy, A Biography*. Lincoln: University of Nebraska Press, 1998.

Peterson, Martin, and Randy Stapilus. *The Idaho 100*. Carlton, Oreg.: Ridenbaugh Press, 2012.

Pettit, Diane. "To Miner, from Grover Cleveland." *Lewiston Morning Tribune*, September 2, 1990.

Pointer, Larry. *In Search of Butch Cassidy*. Norman: University of Oklahoma Press, 1977.

Ripley, Richard. *The Ridgerunner*. Cambridge, Idaho: Backeddy Books, 1986.

RoadsideAmerica.com. "Montpelier, Idaho: Butch Cassidy Bank Robbery Museum." Accessed June 8, 2019. www.roadsideamerica.com/tip/54805.

Roberts, Carol. "Winter Walk—A Little Kellogg History." Silver Valley Stories. February 6, 2008, accessed June 8, 2019. https://silvervalleystories.blogspot .com/2008/02/winter-walk-little-kellogg-history.html.

Schwantes, Carlos. *In Mountain Shadows: A History of Idaho*. Lincoln: University of Nebraska Press, 1991.

Shallat, Todd. *Secrets of the Magic Valley and Hagerman's Remarkable Horse*. Boise, Idaho: Black Canyon Communications, 2002.

Shoshone Ice Caves. www.shoshoneicecaves.com/about.html.

Singletary, Robert. *Kootenai Chronicles: A History of Kootenai County*. Coeur d'Alene: Museum of North Idaho Press, 1994.

Smith, Dennis. "Icy Visions Take Root in Crevices of Frozen Lava." *Deseret News*, October 7, 1994, accessed June 9, 2019. www.deseretnews.com/article/379899/ICY-VISIONS-TAKE-ROOT-IN-CREVICES-OF-FROZEN-LAVA.html.

Spencer, Keith, and Jan Spencer. *Historical Spirit Lake Idaho and Vicinity*. Coeur d'Alene: Museum of North Idaho Press, 2014.

Stapilus, Randy. *Crossing the Snake*. Carlton, Oreg.: Ridenbaugh Press, 2015.

———. *Outlaw Tales of Idaho*. Guilford, Conn.: Two Dot Press, 2008.

Swayne, Zoa L. *Do Them No Harm!* Caldwell, Idaho: Caxton Press, 2003.

Tales of Eldorado. "Idaho: Idaho Treasure." Accessed June 9, 2019. https://sites.google.com/site/talesofeldorado/idaho/.

Thompson, Jessie, ed. *Early Days in the Forest Service*, vol. 4. Missoula, Mont.: U.S. Department of Agriculture Forest Service, Northwest Region, 1976. Accessed June 8, 2019. https://foresthistory.org/wp-content/uploads/2017/02/EARLY-DAYS-IN-THE-FOREST-SERVICE-vol4.pdf.

Trickey, Erick. "Inside the Story of America's 19th-Century Opiate Addiction." *Smithsonian Magazine*, January 4, 2018, accessed June 8, 2019. www.smithsonianmag.com/history/inside-story-americas-19th-century-opiate-addiction-180967673/#0C2RKrYQjumlA8ko.99.

USDA Forest Service. "Magruder Road Corridor." Accessed June 9, 2019.
www.fs.usda.gov/recarea/nezperceclearwater/recarea/?recid=16482.

Utah.com. "Butch Cassidy." Accessed June 9, 2019. https://utah.com/old-west/
butch-cassidy.

Varley, James F. *Tales of the Tract: The Beginnings of Twin Falls, Idaho and the
Magic Valley.* Twin Falls, Idaho: Big Lost River Press, 2008.

Visit Idaho. "Butch Cassidy Museum at the Bank of Montpelier." Accessed
June 8, 2019. https://visitidaho.org/things-to-do/museums/butch-cassidy
-museum-at-the-bank-of-montpelier/?fbclid=IwAR2hrA0qVRXG9ddJtzslf2
brCb2wNAvlhXPG6JyGLfQ0hjAxJGBfr53L4Gg.

Weeks, Andy. *Ghosts of Idaho's Magic Valley: Hauntings and Lore.* Charleston,
S.C.: Haunted America, 2012.

Welch, Julia Conway. *The Magruder Murders: Coping with Violence on the
Western Frontier.* Helena, Mont.: Falcon Press, 1991.

Western Perspective. "The Seven Devil's Mountains: A Nez Perce Legend."
May 24, 2016, accessed June 3, 2019. www.westernperspective.com/
journal/2016/5/24/the-seven-devils-mountains-a-nez-perce-legend.

White Horse Saloon. https://thewhitehorsesaloon.com/.

Zucker, Robert. *Treasures of the Santa Catalina Mountains: Unraveling the
Legends and History.* Tucson, Ariz.: BZB Publishing, 2014.

INDEX

A

Abrams, Dennis, 120, 121, 122
Ada County, 41, 45, 48
Albion, xviii, 49
Allen, Charles, 110, 111, 112, 113
Altmiller, Jake, 87
Anderson, Tim, 120, 121, 124, 125
Arnold, Ken, 116, 117, 118
Atlanta, 48, 78

B

Bank of Montpelier, 153, 154, 155,
    156, 157, 158, 160, 161, 165
Bannack, 106, 109, 110, 113, 169,
    170
Bannock tribe, 119, 169
Beachey, Hill, 107, 109, 114, 115
Bear Lake, xix, 26, 28, 29, 30, 31, 33,
    34, 36, 37, 154, 158, 160, 163, 164
Bear Lake Monster, xix, 26, 30, 31,
    34, 36, 37
Bear River, 28, 29
Bellevue, 144, 152

Bethmann, Emilie, 69, 71, 74
Bethmann family, 68, 69, 72, 73, 74
Bethmann, Frieda, 69, 70, 71, 72, 74
Bethmann, Harry, 70, 71
Bethmann, Miner, 71, 72
Big Creek, vii, 76
Bigfoot, xv
Big River Paranormal, 129, 138
Bill the donkey, 90, 95, 97, 101
Bitterroot Mountains, 16, 17, 19, 22,
    23, 79, 82, 103, 104, 106, 110, 169
Blackfeet, 18, 21, 23
Blackfoot, 119, 144
Blackwell, Frank, 57
Blake, True and Dennis, 94
Boise, xi, xvii, xx, 1, 2, 3, 4, 5, 6, 8, 9,
    10, 11, 40, 41, 44, 45, 47, 48, 116,
    129, 130, 131, 132, 134, 138, 161,
    171
Boise River, 45, 91, 129, 132
Bonner County, xvi
Bonners Ferry, 50, 52
Brockie Jack, 41, 44, 45, 48
Brooklyn Ann, 60

About the Author

Randy Stapilus is an author, blogger, newsletter publisher, and former newspaper reporter and editor. He also has written *It Happened in Idaho*, *Speaking Ill of the Dead: Jerks in Idaho History*, and *Outlaw Tales of Idaho* for Globe Pequot Press, among other books. A longtime Idaho resident, he now lives in Carlton, Oregon, with his wife Linda, and a varying number of dogs.